The Holocaust and the Press:

Nazi War Crimes Trials in Germany and Israel

The Hampton Press Communication Series
Political Communication
David L. Paletz, Editor

The Holocaust and the Press:
Nazi War Crimes Trials in Germany and Israel

Akiba A. Cohen
Tel Aviv University

Tamar Zemach-Marom
The JDC-Brookdale Institute

Jürgen Wilke
Johannes Gutenberg University

Birgit Schenk
Johannes Gutenberg University

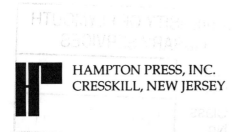

HAMPTON PRESS, INC.
CRESSKILL, NEW JERSEY

Copyright © 2002 by Hampton Press, Inc.

Printed in the United States of America

Library of Congress Cataloging-in-Publication Data

Cohen, Akiba A.
    The Holocaust and the Press: Nazi War Crimes Trials in Germany and Israel / Akiba A. Cohen ... [et al.].
        p. cm. -- (The Hampton Press communication series)
    Includes bibliographical references and index.
    ISBN 1-58283-387-X -- ISBN 1-57273-388-8 (pbk.)
    1. Holocaust, Jewish (1939-1945)--Mass media and the Holocaust. 2. Holocaust, Jewish (1939-1945)--Press coverage--Germany. 3. Holocaust, Jewish (1939-1945)--Press coverage--Israel. 4. War crime trials--Press coverage--Germany. 5. War crime trials--press coverage Israel. I. Series.

D804.3.C62 2001
940.53'18--dc21

                                                                2001046333

Cover art: Chava Pressburger
Cover design: Buddy Boy Design

Hampton Press, Inc.
23 Broadway
Cresskill, NJ 07626

Contents

Acknowledgments

The study described in this volume is a joint Israeli-German project. The idea to examine the press coverage of Nazi war crimes that took place in the two countries was developed in Israel in the early 1990s. Despite the fact that the subject of the Holocaust has special meaning for understanding the self-identity of both Germans and Israelis, little research has been done on the topic, especially at the comparative bi-national level.

From the start the project encountered some major difficulties and required much effort from both national research teams. Thanks to generous funding, the volume of material that became available for analysis was enormous. From time to time there were problems of coordination between the two teams; hence the researchers conducted two lengthy seminars, one in Jerusalem and one in Mainz, to iron out the difficulties.

The project received financial support from the German National Center for Political Education (Bundeszentrale für politische Bildung) that has been active for quite a number of years and has developed firm relations with Israel, including the active training of journalists. The idea to support the project was first raised by the Center's former director, Wolfgang Maurus, during a visit to Israel by a delegation representing the Center in March 1991, shortly after the Gulf War. We wish to thank the Center, not only for its support of the study by also for helping to disseminate it. An earlier book, funded by the Center, published in German in 1995 by Böhlau Verlag of Cologne, provided the main edifice for the current volume. The German version was naturally written from a German Perspective with the German reader in mind. Although the current English version contains essentially the same data as the German version, it is not merely a translation of the earlier volume. Instead, it is a new and enhanced text, which we believe will be more pertinent for non-German readers.

Professors Cohen and Wilke directed the study. Dr. Zemach-Marom did her doctoral dissertation at the Hebrew University of Jerusalem on the Israeli part of the study.

This study would not have been possible without the many people who assisted us, especially our student coders. On the German side, we wish to mention Monika Britz, Claudia Deeg, Antje Fritz, Christine Gräf, Angela Hennersdorf, Angela Majewski, Berit Paflik, and Markus Schöberl. In Israel, credit is due to Einav Bar, Orlee Cohen, Amir Dan, Eran Etan, Naomi Fassa, Arik Feldman, Aviva Frankel, Ari Geva, Anna Gingichashvilli, Liat Hamburger, Arlie Lipsky, Arie Manos, Yosef Markowitz, Yifat Reuveni, Ganela Rubinstein, Inbar Sharav, Almog Sharav, and Gal Shai. We also with to give special thanks to two people in Mainz: Ralph Bartel who helped with the statistical analyses and Andreas Czaplicki for his consultation and support. Finally, Sivan Schejter and Noa Loffler-Elefant helped with various tasks when preparing this English version.

We would also like to express our appreciation to Barbara Bernstein, president of Hampton Press for her interest in the English book and to Professor David Paletz, editor of the series at Hampton, for his encouragement.

Last but not least, we wish to thank each other for the friendship and cooperation throughout the years of the project. We could not do it without each other.

AAC, TZM, JW, and BS
July 2001

1

The Holocaust and Nazi War Crimes Trials in Retrospect

Looking back at the previous century, there is little doubt that the extermination of European Jewry by Nazi Germany was one of the most shocking and incomprehensible events of the modern era. The attempt to eradicate an entire people in a well-planned and calculated fashion was something virtually unprecedented in human history. The machinery set in motion during the 1930s reached its climax and perfection during the Second World War. Curiously, however, very few detailed reports on the atrocities were published in the press of those days (Lipstadt, 1986), not by newspapers of the Allied forces, not by the Jewish press in Palestine, and certainly not in Germany.

Only after the war did the details begin to come to light. The Allied soldiers freeing the concentration camps were shocked facing the remnants of the monstrosities that took place behind the barbed wire fences. Years later, research shed more light and understanding as to what happened. An important source was the testimonies of those who lived to tell it, perpetrators and survivors alike. Some of these accounts were heard in trials of Nazi war criminals. The coverage of the trials in the media made it possible for the general public to be exposed to the horrible stories. In a strange way, past events became news because, as noted, at the time they were actually happening, they were not reported.

1

Being such a momentous event, the task of coming to grips with the Holocaust was tackled by different viewpoints and methods. First and foremost, it necessitated a systematic uncovering of what actually had occurred. This task was primarily that of scientific historical research. The Holocaust has even become the subject of its own encyclopedia. However, historical research concerned with precise facts, obtained from printed, recorded, and filmed documents, was only one of many approaches to the subject.

The research presented in this volume is based on a longitudinal study of the manner in which the daily press in Israel and in Germany dealt with the subject of the Holocaust. The study focuses on four periods, each centering on a major war crimes trial: the Nuremberg trial (1945-46) held in Nuremberg, Germany; the Eichmann trial (1961) in Jerusalem, Israel; the Auschwitz trial (1963-65) in Frankfurt, Germany; and the Demjanjuk trial (1987-88), also in Jerusalem.

The decision to focus on the trials is based on the assumption that in the course of everyday life, there are, from time to time, events that awaken issues latent in the public mind and that are peripheral to the news. This is especially true of historic events that have social significance, but that do not attract great attention or do not stand out in the public eye over long periods of times. Such past events do not usually interest the press, which by its journalistic news values tends to concentrate on contemporary events—at least until some current event provides a context in which events of the past come to the fore. The Holocaust is an excellent example of a central historical topic that has contemporary relevance to society and therefore justifies the present-oriented press in bringing it up on certain occasions. Thus Nazi war crimes trials have brought the subject of the Holocaust back to public awareness, laid it out from time to time on the public agenda, and forced the public to deal with it.

According to the "agenda-setting hypothesis" (McCombs & Shaw, 1972), topics targeted and focused on by the mass media will be perceived as important by media consumers; thus the media priorities are transformed into the agenda of the public. According to this theory, the point at which the media bring the topics to light for the first time has the greatest impact on the public. Inasmuch as the Holocaust was not brought to the public's awareness in real time, when the events transpired, media interest, from time to time, as each new trial got underway, was likely to have brought the topic back again.

Focusing on the trials is important not only because it brings an historical subject to the public agenda but also because it can shed light on more subtle processes such as creating national conflict or consensus, as the case may be. In this light one can assess the debate arising from time to time as to whether Nazi war criminals should be brought to trial altogether. Another issue that came up was the fact that the trials serve as an opportunity to do justice not only with regard to a single person but to express sentiments towards a people and an entire era. Thus this debate is part of the broader question of whether or not the subject of the Holocaust should be continuously discussed. This dilemma arose, for example, during the Demjanjuk trial in Israel and the Zundel trial in Canada (Weimann & Winn, 1986). Therefore, the way such trials were covered by the press should be studied carefully. A preliminary analysis of the subject shows that the coverage of the various trials by the press was different both in terms of quantity and format.

Social scientists, like many others, have been continuously trying to understand the reasons for the atrocities committed by the Nazis. They have been less interested in the question of *what* happened (a question that historians deal with) but rather in the question of *how* and *why* such events *could have* happened. Nazi war crimes trials could shed light on this question. Bosch (1970) addressed this issue in dealing with the Nuremberg trial, claiming that it served as a special opportunity to study psychological and sociological factors characterizing the modern world, including the relationship between personality and power, the role of the individual in the hierarchy of modern bureaucracy, the dynamics of the totalitarian state, mass psychology, and the influence of propaganda on cultural and ethical norms.

This wide array of subjects arising, at least partially, in Nazi war crimes trials, found its way to the media in general and particularly to the printed press. On the research level, however, despite the overall importance of empirical data, especially on such highly charged topics as the Holocaust, which are more susceptible to researcher bias, the little research done on news coverage of the trials has been impressionistic and lacked an empirical base. This is another reason to attempt a systematic investigation relying on hard empirical data.

Moreover, when considering the way the Israeli and German societies dealt with their collective memory of the Holocaust, it turned out that the subject is multifaceted and highly complex. Dealing with the Holocaust took many forms over the years, and although much has been written on this topic, it took a relatively long time before empirical studies were undertaken.

The Holocaust has been an open wound. Just as survivor and author Yehiel Dinur (alias *Katzetnick*) referred to the Holocaust as "another planet," so it might be appropriate to speak of "another planet of inquiry." Whereas in Israel there has been virtually no research on public opinion relating to the Holocaust, in Germany there has been some research in this area (see Chapter 3). Furthermore, there are no comparative and longitudinal data available on public opinion that might reveal how the public dealt with the memory of the Holocaust; thus researchers must resort to various sources, including records and documents. One such possible source is the press. Surely, newspapers *themselves* cannot be considered as reliable sources of public opinion. However, few would deny that in the second half of the twentieth century the press has been a central element in the fabric of society, and therefore can serve as a reliable and valid source for *presenting* and *interpreting* public opinion.

Nir and Roeh (1992) claim that the rationale for longitudinal study of press coverage in different newspapers is based on the assumption that the press can tell how society perceives itself and constructs its worldview. Hence, the role that the press plays in representing the period in which it was published makes it possible to include it among other historical-social documents and it is fundamentally no different from them. Moreover, according to Startt and Sloan (1989) an historical picture constructed without taking the media into consideration would be distorted. The mass media of the past are part of that period and cannot be uprooted, thus providing historians with valuable insight. The media are part of the building blocks of modern life; they are a rich historical source and hence deserve serious consideration. Israeli historian and journalist Tom Segev (1994a) also stressed the importance of the press as an historical source and claimed that any historian relying on the Israeli press would know almost everything about the society at any given point in time. There is no need to enter the debate as to the nature of media influence or the scope of its impact. Even those who argue that the press only mirrors societal beliefs cannot deny the importance of analyzing what appears in the media.

The present study is probably the first attempt of its kind to provide a comprehensive and systematic picture concerning the longitudinal changes in the press coverage of the Holocaust. It should be noted that newspapers are the only mass medium that existed since the end of World War II whose contents are available for current analysis (although radio did exist, recordings of programs are generally unavailable and television was in its infancy). Moreover, newspapers have a special status in fulfilling the public's communication needs. According to the "uses and gratifications" approach to media research, people have a complex system of needs that they seek to fulfill through the mass media. Katz and Gurevitch (1973), who compared five different mass media (newspaper, books, radio, television and film), found that newspapers are the most important medium in fulfilling peoples' needs; namely, the need for stability and personal security, social status, deepening knowledge, and understanding of society and the world in general.

The messages transmitted by the media are often referred to in the literature as "symbolic reality" (Adoni & Mane, 1984). This term does not include only news items, the purpose of which is to provide information. This dissemination of knowledge is supplemented by laying out the background, presenting specialists' opinions, and feedback from media consumers. One of the most profound methods for studying the symbolic reality is content analysis. Symbolic reality is not necessarily identical with the "objective" reality that people experience as the world around them and to which they refer as facts. The third kind of reality is the "subjective social reality," where the symbolic and objective realities converge and create a new reality, from the viewpoint of the individual.

Molotch and Lester (1974) as well as numerous other scholars over the years deny the very existence of the objective world that is the essence of news reports. They maintain that the process of making news is one of socially constructing reality by those who have power and vested interests. Further, it is argued, there is no such thing as objective reporting, or mirroring of the world, or passive copying of events. Everything said, photographed, or written will come from a certain perspective, which is rooted in a specific time and place.

The relations between symbolic reality and subjective reality stirred a heated debate as to the validity of the "cultivation hypothesis." Gerbner and Gross (1976), the main proponents of this hypothesis, held that the messages of mass media provide a uniform way for perceiving and understanding the world. They showed that there was a moderate positive correlation between the amount of television viewing and the perception of credibility of television in presenting the "real" world, or in other words, between the exposure to symbolic reality and the construction of one's subjective social reality. They found in their studies a positive correlation between the extent of television exposure and beliefs as to the rate of violence existing in reality and the perceived likelihood of being victimized in the "real" world. Opponents of this view (e.g., Doob & Macdonald, 1979) base their argument on theoretical as well as statistical-empirical grounds. They deny the existence of such a relationship and claim that the correlation decreases as control for certain variables are introduced.

As for the Holocaust, there is evidence concerning the importance of the media in creating subjective social reality. For example, in a study by Farago (1984) the mass media were the main source of influence on adolescents' perception of the Holocaust. However, even here, it should be noted that the influence of the media is not exclusive. Moreover, it can go in both directions: on the one hand the media influence perceptions and on the other hand they reflect what the public thinks and feels. The message must be framed in terms understood and accepted by the public. As a rule, the media present ideas that are positively accepted by their audience and reject ideas that are not accepted. Ryan (1991) follows this line of thought, suggesting that this process involves framing bits of information into a meaningful story for the public and writers alike. The process includes the selection of events perceived as important for the issue at hand. It seems that the study of the message—the product of this selection process—has merit even without studying the question of direction of influence from the media to the public or vice versa.

Given the nature and importance of these four trials, they all received considerable press coverage. Some of the reporting touched upon problematic issues pertaining to the trials themselves. Some of the issues were concerned with possible pretrial judgments and others were about the use of cameras in the courtrooms and turning the legal proceedings into show trials. This argument was made particularly with regard to the Eichmann and Demjanjuk trials, both of which took place not in regular Jerusalem courtrooms but in theater auditoriums especially converted into courtrooms for the purpose of the trials.

The complex and delicate dilemma concerning the role of the press in reporting from the courtroom is not new and has been exacerbated in the television era. The principles of freedom of the press and fair trial are not always compatible. Rivers (1975) raised the question as to whether the press in a democratic society, while exercising its guarantees of free speech, including making comments and expressing opinions about the guilt or innocence of defendants, are in fact not jeopardizing a fair trial. In some democratic societies, jurors can be sequestered (or at least ordered by the presiding judge(s) to refrain from exposing themselves to media coverage of their case) so as to prevent them from being influenced by what is published and broadcast. Other democratic societies have *sub-judice* laws totally prohibiting most pretrial discussion of impending cases even when professional judges, rather than jurors, are used.

Allowing cameras in the courtroom has been a controversial issue in many countries and is done only on rare occasions. The law forbidding pictures in a courtroom was first implemented in the United States in 1935 as a protest against the circus atmosphere in the trial of Bruno Hauptmann, who was found guilty of kidnapping and murdering the Lindbergh child (Hohenberg, 1969). Bringing cameras into the courtroom is still controversial in some states in America. The rationale for the prohibition is that public attention derived from media coverage might create prejudice against defendants. Presiding judges warn against the interference of the media during the trial, noting that the defendant has the right to stand trial in court but is not required to stand trial before the general public. Trials are not like elections, they warn, and one cannot manage them properly in auditoriums or on radio or television. There have even been cases of convictions being overturned on appeal on grounds of prior judgment by the press where the U.S. Supreme Court accepted the argument that the media deprived the defendants of a fair trial (Hohenberg, 1969).

In a specific case in Israel, related to the Demjanjuk trial, Noah Kliger, a journalist at *Yedioth Aharonoth* was convicted for violating Israel's *sub-judice* law, because of certain items that appeared in his newspaper "convicting" Demjanjuk before he had a chance to prove his innocence in court.

As in the case of the Eichmann trial, the complaint that Israel was conducting a show trial came up once again during the Demjanjuk trial and was widely debated in the media. During this trial television had already existed in Israel for two decades and the trial was broadcast live from the courtroom. On many occasions the evening news showed selected segments from the day's session.

Even if these trials should not have been deemed as show trials, they might still be referred to as media events, as defined by Dayan and Katz (1992). Media events are ceremonial events, broadcast live, well prepared ahead of time and accompanied by a well-organized pre-publication. They enable the audience to participate in the event and even may lead to the reunion of society. Some media events serve the function of memory; they remind what is worth to remember. They are also "electronic monuments" that are supposed to live in the collective memory via their connection to the traumas of which the events are a reaction or through the satisfaction they provide. Media events, according to Katz and Dayan, edit the collective memory time and time again, often having a similar role to that of a religious holiday. By doing so they create a genre dedicated to such special occasions.

The expectation that certain events will become media events is the proof that there is public awareness of the genre. During the Demjanjuk trial, for example, there were people who appealed to the Israeli Supreme Court demanding that the trial be broadcast live. Nazi war crimes trials in general and the Eichmann trial in particular got special attention by the media and the public and were related to past traumatic events. In later trials, like the Demjanjuk trial, there was an additional layer of relating to past events: not only to events of the Holocaust but to similar media events, such as the frequent mentioning of the Eichmann trial itself.

2

The Trials and Their
Journalistic Context

Following the collapse of the Third Reich, an immediate review of Nazi war crimes had begun. German courts were initially part of the process but were limited to dealing with crimes committed against Germans by Germans. In fact, until 1950, only the Allied forces that occupied Germany were authorized to prosecute people accused of committing crimes against non-Germans.

In the Federal Republic of Germany, preliminary investigations against nearly 104,000 people were carried out between November 30, 1945 and January 1, 1992, and a total of 6,487 people were tried, convicted, and sentenced (Grabitz, 1994). Although immediately at the end of the war thousands of investigations and criminal proceedings were instituted, the number of cases decreased markedly during the 1950s. Only after the Central Office of the National Judiciary Authority for the Resolution of Nazi Crimes of Violence had begun its work in Ludwigsburg in 1958 did the number of investigations and judgments noticeably increase again (Kruse, 1978).

The four trials dealt with in this study of course only comprise a fraction of the total number of potentially relevant trials. They do, however, unquestionably belong to the small group of trials that engendered the greatest attention worldwide. Two of these trials took place on German soil: the Nuremberg trial against the so-called "chief war criminals" and the Auschwitz trial in Frankfurt. The trials against the other two accused, Adolf Eichmann and Ivan Demjanjuk, were conducted in

Israel. It should be noted that all trials in Israel are presided over and decided by professional judges and not by juries. In Germany, on the other hand, criminal trials use the jury system.

Following is a brief review of the four trials as well as the conditions and circumstances of their journalistic reporting.

THE NUREMBERG TRIAL

The political leaders of the victorious Allies decided at a relatively early stage that the Nazi leadership and those chiefly responsible for the war and its reign of terror should be held accountable (Weber, 1968). In the Moscow Declaration of November 1, 1943, Roosevelt, Churchill, and Stalin signed an agreement whereby people who took part in Nazi war crimes would be tried in the countries in which the crimes were committed. Excluded from this requirement were the so-called "chief war criminals," whose crimes were not localized to a specific geographical area. Instead, Article 1 of the London Four-Power Agreement of August 8, 1945 specifically stated that the pursuit and prosecution of the chief war criminals of the European Axis be carried out by an international military tribunal.

The International Court of Military Justice first convened in Berlin on October 18, 1945 to accept this charge, which covered four counts: (a) crimes against peace; that is, the planning, initiating, and waging of war in violation of international treaties and agreements; (b) crimes against humanity; that is, extermination, deportation, and genocide; (c) war crimes; that is, violations of the laws of war; and (d) conspiracy to commit the crimes listed in the first three counts. Although the first two counts were drafted mainly by the British and American prosecution authorities, the French and the Soviets were involved in the formulation of the latter two counts. The prosecution was directed at 25 chief war criminals specified by name as well as towards the following Nazi groups and organizations: the SS, SA, SD, Gestapo, the government of the Reich, the corps of political functionaries, the General Staff, and the High Command of the German Wehrmacht.

The Nuremberg trial began on November 20, 1945 in the Palace of Justice in Nuremberg. Of the 25 accused, three did not appear before the court: the former head of the Reich's labor organization, Robert Ley, committed suicide while in custody; the industrialist Gustav Krupp was determined "unfit to stand trial"; and Martin Bormann, Hitler's secretary and the former head of Rudolf Hess' staff office, managed to flee. Also, Kaltenbrunner was absent at the beginning of the trial but later joined the other defendants. The court, presided over by the British Lord

Justice Geoffrey Lawrence, consisted of a representative of each of the four victorious Powers and their deputies. Each of the four Powers also provided a chief prosecutor and a number of assistant prosecutors.

The trial ended on October 1, 1946. It took the court two days to pronounce its judgments: twelve death sentences were handed down; seven defendants received prison terms; and three were acquitted. Those condemned to death were executed the following day. Göring avoided execution by committing suicide in his jail cell.

Several subsequent trials held in Nuremberg, including the so-called "doctor's trial," the "lawyer's trial," and the "Wilhelmstrasse trial" have been controversial among many historians and jurists. The allied Powers had indeed pursued their goal, including holding the representatives of the Nazi regime personally responsible, but the trials served primarily as an intellectual examination of and reckoning with Nazi ideology. This led to what Rückerl (1979) characterized as a predominance of discussions of political events. Accordingly, war crimes and crimes against humanity faded in importance and occasionally retreated entirely into the background. In reporting the trials, political, military, and criminal events were somehow mixed together, so that it became very difficult for an impartial observer seeking a clear picture to unravel the tangles. The interest of the German people in the trials seemed to wane as the proceedings went on (Merritt & Merritt, 1970) because of the extensive discussions of legal issues such as retroactive legislation and the application of legal principles regarding crimes against humanity and peace.

Another outstanding goal of the Nuremberg trial was the repeated resolve of the Allies to create new, internationally binding legal principles, thereby preventing any comparable future crimes and punishing any such legal violations. However, according to Weber (1968), the meaning of the Nuremberg trial lay not in the international sphere, for its principles anticipated in part a not-yet-existing order, but was confined to Germany. This was because the trials were limited to the former German elite, and could have no detrimental effect on a future German State, as indicated in the Treaty of Versailles. Thus there was no collective condemnation of the entire German people.

The Allies were determined that the Nuremberg trial would resonate with the international public. Explicitly by means of the publicity with which it was carried out, an enlightening and deterring effect, indeed a catharsis, was intended. To this end a multitude of journalists were invited to cover the trials in the press and radio (television was not yet available). In fact, 240 seats in the Nuremberg Palace of Justice were designated for reporters. In addition, the proceedings were broadcast via loudspeakers to an adjacent pressroom (Taylor, 1992). The foreign journalists were put up in one of the castles near Nuremberg. Commentators and reporters from more than 20 countries gathered there: roughly 80 from the United States, 50 from the United Kingdom, 40 from France, 35 from the Soviet Union, 20 from Poland, and a dozen or so from Czechoslovakia. Among them could be found (subsequently) famous names like Walter Cronkite, William L. Shirer, Peter de Mendelssohn, Ilya Ehrenburg, and Markus Wolf, who later became the head of the Foreign Intelligence Department of the former German Democratic Republic (East Germany).

There were also several reporters from the German press. As yet, as noted earlier, most of the studies dealing with the press coverage of Nazi war crimes trials were based on impressions and interpretations rather than on systematic content analyses. This includes, for example, the claim made by Steinbach (1984), without basis in empirical evidence, that there was little coverage of the Nuremberg trial in the German press.

From the perspective of the Allies and the prosecution team, one of the primary reasons for conducting the Nuremberg trial was the desire to confront the German public with what had occurred during the war. This task was made easier given the fact that at the time of the trials newspapers in Germany had to be licensed by the Allies. In addition, there were direct forms of allied control of the press through which not only could undesired articles be prevented, but the desired portrayal and presentation could be ensured.

Koszyk (1986) described the care that the American Information Control Division gave to the reporting of the Nuremberg trial. Koszyk indicates that on September 13, 1945, General McClure ordered that the licensed newspapers be provided with extra paper for double-sided supplements. On November 5th the Deutsche Allgemeine Nachrichtenagentur (German General Press Agency), which had the monopoly for the reporting on the trials, revised its guidelines for the licensed press. Thereafter, the ban on Nazi and military propaganda, formulated in early September 1945, no longer applied to statements by witnesses and the defense, but did apply to commentary on the trials. Commentaries could discuss the development of the proceedings as long as they did not touch upon the role and function of the court or predict the verdicts. The accused could neither be designated as "criminals" nor could they be ridiculed. In this delicate context the licensed press was obliged to provide "objective" news and restrained commentary.

Further instructions of this sort followed, with the British being the most restrained. However, according to Koszyk (1986) the French were less hesitant. Koszyk describes the French General Administrator as saying that two German journalists were to be admitted to the

Nuremberg tribunal under surveillance by the representative of the Information Office, that their written and designated articles would be distributed by the Zone Agency and would be published in all newspapers. Furthermore, every edition should leave space for the reporting of the trials but care should be taken so that readers would not grow weary and the impression of massive propaganda was to be avoided. General Laffont even recommended specific topics to be emphasized and spoke of a "trial by humanity against nihilism." He also directed the Censorship Commission to make available the newsprint necessary for the reports.

During the time that the Nuremberg trial was conducted, the Jewish press in Palestine also existed under unusual conditions. The state of Israel had not yet been established and Palestine was still a British mandate. Under these political conditions free journalistic operation was likewise restricted, quite apart from financial problems that made it impossible for Jewish-owned Hebrew newspapers—with the exception of the *Ha'aretz* daily—to send their own correspondents to Germany.

THE EICHMANN TRIAL

Next to the Nuremberg trial, the 1961 trial of Adolf Eichmann created the greatest worldwide sensation. Eichmann had been Head of the Jewish Department in the Imperial Security Administration of the Reich and therefore had overall responsibility for the implementation of the "final solution" for the Jewish "problem." Indeed, it is said that Eichmann once remarked that he would joyfully jump into his grave, because the knowledge that five million Jews were on his conscience gave him a feeling of great satisfaction.

After the war, Eichmann, like other Nazi officers, fled to Argentina and went underground. Although Eichmann's place of residence was known, no country had demanded his extradition. In May 1960 Eichmann was tracked down by the Israeli *Mossad* and was abducted from Buenos Aires to Israel. By so doing Israel had taken the initiative to bring to trial one of the criminals chiefly responsible for the murder of several million people.

The abduction of Adolf Eichmann—contrary to international law—was not the only circumstance regarding his subsequent trial that seemed to be judicially problematic. Putting Eichmann on trial on the basis of a law passed in 1950 by the Knesset (the Israeli parliament), which was applied retroactively, for the "punishment of Nazis and Nazi helpers" came under criticism (Papadatos, 1964) despite the fact that precedents for retroactive legislation were already set in the Nuremberg trial.

And yet, nobody seriously disputed Israel's right to bring Eichmann to justice. His trial took place from April 11 to December 15, 1961 in a special chamber of the Jerusalem district court, converted from a theater auditorium. Under a three-judge panel presided over by judge Moshe Landau, the trial became a lesson in contemporary history, in which the person of the accused seemed to play only a relatively minor role. The strategy of the trial, led by the prosecutor, Israel's Attorney General Gideon Hausner, was aimed at bringing to light the overall historical events of the "final solution" and the role played by the defendant in the process.

To this end, hundreds of witnesses were called to testify about the details of the machinery of annihilation, thereby documenting Eichmann's personal guilt. Eichmann's German defense lawyer, especially approved by the court (generally, non-Israeli lawyers cannot appear before Israeli courts) had already appeared as a lawyer during the Nuremberg trial, claimed that his client was "not guilty in the sense of the accusation." Eichmann, the defense claimed, did not personally order any murders, let alone commit any. Nevertheless, Eichmann did not deny the crimes cited in the indictment, but he denied any personal responsibility, because as an "obedient civil servant" he was only following orders "from above." These defense strategies raised interesting legal questions concerning individual responsibility and wrongful orders.

The conduct of Eichmann's Jewish victims during the war also became a controversial issue in the context of the trial. This polemic was provoked mainly in the depiction of the trial by the Jewish German philosopher and political scientist Hannah Arendt, who reported from Jerusalem in a series of articles in the *New Yorker Magazine*, which were later published in book form as *Eichmann in Jerusalem: A Report on the Banality of Evil* (Arendt, 1963). Arendt viewed Eichmann as a "dumb bureaucrat," hence she spoke of the "banality of evil" and doubted whether the Nazis could have succeeded in murdering so many people without the passivity of the rest of the world and the collaboration of the Jewish leadership. On December 11, 1961 the court sentenced Adolf Eichmann to death, a sentence upheld by the Israel Supreme Court on May 29, 1962 (Less, 1987). Eichmann was hanged two days later, his body was cremated, and his ashes were scattered in the Mediterranean so that there would be no permanent gravesite for him.

As one of the goals of the young State of Israel was to demonstrate to the world public through the Eichmann trial that Israel would demand reckoning for the crimes committed by the Nazi regime against the Jews, great importance was attached to covering and reporting the trial. Extensive preparations were made to ensure smooth work for over 400 journalists from numerous countries who were present—at least at the beginning of the trial. Diplomats and official observers were also present, among them some from the Federal Republic of Germany as well as representatives of international organizations.

At the time of the Eichmann trial there was no television service in Israel, so the general question of permitting TV cameras in courtrooms was not an issue (television began in Israel only in 1968). However, this did not prevent this specific trial from being carried live via closed circuit television to a large nearby auditorium and pictures of the defendant, who sat throughout the proceedings in a bulletproof glass booth, were shown on a large screen. The video material was also made available to any interested broadcasting service to be aired around the world. It should be noted that as a rule, cameras are still not allowed in Israeli courtrooms.

In her description of the Eichmann trial, Arendt (1963) also recounted the physical setting of the courtroom. She indicated that the participants sat on the stage as if they were in a play and that they entered the stage through the side doors normally designated for the actors. In a way, Arendt continues, the "stage manager" of the Eichmann trial was David Ben-Gurion, the Prime Minister of Israel. Although he did not appear in court, he spoke through Hausner's (the prosecutor's) mouth, who made numerous theatrical gestures. Hausner even gave Ben-Gurion an advance copy of his opening statement, seeking his comments. The opening of the trial, according to Segev (1993), signified that the judicial process was not the main thing; instead, it was designed to create an emotional spectacle more than it was aimed at broadening knowledge. The participants-witnesses were allowed to talk at great length almost without interruption by the prosecutor, as if they were reciting their parts in the play (Arendt, 1963). Haim Guri, an Israeli author and poet, also admitted that at times he felt as if he was in the theater: "at one or two moments an atmosphere of a fair or theater hovered in the hall until the bailiff's voice was heard, the judges came in, bowed gently to the public who rose in their honor" (Guri, 1963, p. 191). Elsewhere Guri notes: "every courtroom resembles a theater sometimes. Along with its seriousness you can find in it some aspects of a play" (p. 176).

Some of the press also supported this assertion. On March 22, 1961 the Israeli daily *Ha'aretz* came out with the headline: "The Eichmann Circus." Elsewhere there were phrases such as: "The Curtain Went Up" (*Hatzofeh*, April 12, 1961) or "The Curtain Falls" (*Hatzofeh*, December 17, 1961). Also, prosecutor Hausner, in an unusual move, was permitted to give television interviews and to appear at press conferences.

Robinson (1965) refuted Arendt's arguments one by one. He maintained that the legal procedures in Israel were internationally acceptable, that Hausner did not convene a formal press conference during the trial, and that the prosecution as well as the defense kept informal ties with the press. Robinson also argued with Arendt concerning the theatrical nature of the trial by citing various opinions attesting to the fact that the prosecutor was a legal expert with high professional standards.

Hausner (1968), in his own book *The Jerusalem Trial*, also refuted the accusation that he cooperated in conducting a show trial. He described how a senior official approached him after the first day of trial—when the legal aspects of the trial were being raised by the defense—voicing his fear that a lengthy reply by the prosecution would bore the journalists, most of whom were scheduled to remain in Israel for only one week. The official allegedly said: "think what they will write in their newspapers," thereby expressing his concern that dull legal points would turn the public away from the trial. The Israeli press also attacked Hausner, claiming that this was not the way to start a historical trial. Hausner replied, however, by saying, "This is a trial, not a show," and claimed he was not affected by it.

Several studies were conducted on the press coverage of the Eichmann trial, but here, too, without a solid empirical base. One notable exception was the study conducted by the Institute of Human Relations (1962) in which editorials from approximately 2,000 American newspapers were examined. The study concluded that most of the editorials did not focus on the atrocities but rather on the broader significance of the trial to the world and specifically to the American people. One of the dominant themes was that distinguishing between good and evil lies with the individual and that one couldn't avoid responsibility by claiming to have fulfilled orders. Numerous newspapers claimed that not only was Eichmann guilty but that all of Western society neglected its moral obligations. The criticism and blame was directed towards the entire world and not towards Germany alone as responsible for the Nazis coming to power. Eichmann's image in the press was of an arch-fiend and a sadist symbolizing the entire period.

A similar view was espoused by Sontag (1966), who argued that Eichmann the man was sentenced for his personal crimes whereas Eichmann the symbol was sentenced for the destruction of European Jewry, if not for the entire history of anti-Semitism. It was also an attempt to turn the incomprehensible into something meaningful. Sontag found that on the opening day of the trial there was at least one editorial in all daily newspapers in the United States, but that this close attention did not repeat itself even on the day following Eichmann's conviction. According to Glock, Selznick, and Spaeth (1966), the Eichmann trial reached the American public only via the mass media and that one of its great successes was the extent of coverage it had received, both quantitatively and qualitatively.

Everyone concerned with the Eichmann trial agreed that the Israeli press covered the trial in unprecedented detail. Keren (1985) noted that the broad press coverage of the trial imposed great responsibility on the journalists. They were the ones who had to choose what to present to the public from the tremendous amount of details. Segev (1994a) suggested that the press discovered the Holocaust as a journalistic story. Behind this change lies the realization that readers were interested in the topic and wanted to read about it. Supporting evidence to this claim of change of attitude comes to light when comparing the coverage of the Eichmann trial to that of the trials of several "Kapos" (Jews accused of aiding the Nazis) during the 1950s. At that time, the subject was hardly mentioned, but after the Eichmann trial, when the trial of another "Kapo" (the Hirshberg trial) was held, it was covered widely by the press.

The Israeli press emphasized the importance of the trial as a means of raising awareness to the subject and influencing world public opinion. The press was united in its support of Israel's right to bring Eichmann to trial (Hausner, 1968) and some journalists even wrote that he should be executed. A day after Eichmann's capture was announced, the Israeli daily *Ma'ariv* declared: "Only one possible ruling for a mass murderer: Death." Nobody paid attention to the appeal by the minister of justice to respect the *sub-judice* law (Segev, 1993). Every important event in the trial caused immediate speculations in the press as to its potential effect on public opinion. Editorials sometimes voiced doubts just in order to protect the legitimacy of Israel's actions (Glock et al., 1966). According to Guttman (as quoted by Keren, 1985) the press sometimes preferred sensationalism to serious discussion about the meaning and consequences of the Holocaust.

Following Israel, the greatest amount of attention given to the Eichmann trial was in West Germany (Carmichael, 1961). More West German reporters were sent to cover the trial than from any other country. The newspapers did not hide the facts that were revealed in the trial and most of them devoted at least one editorial to the trial. They made a concerted effort to separate between the Eichmann trial and the political atmosphere at the time.

THE AUSCHWITZ TRIAL

Two years after the Eichmann trial, another Nazi war crimes trial that drew considerable attention took place in Germany. Officially referred to as the Criminal Proceedings Against Mulka and Others, the Auschwitz trial in Frankfurt was one of the longest jury trials in the history of German jurisprudence.

In 1958, a former Auschwitz prisoner, incarcerated at the time in Bruchsal, complained to the authorities against Wilhelm Boger, who had been a prison guard at the Auschwitz concentration camp in Poland during the Nazi regime. As the German authorities did not respond to his accusations, he turned to Hermann Langbein, the general secretary of the International Auschwitz Committee in Vienna, Austria. Langbein turned the matter over to the Central Office of the National Judiciary Authority for the Prosecution of Nazi Crimes of Violence in Ludwigsburg, which had begun its work at the end of 1958. In the course of their investigations, officials turned up a number of other people who, like Boger, had committed crimes in Auschwitz.

After more than five years of discovery and preparation for the trial the main proceedings took twenty months. When the trial opened on December 20, 1963 in Frankfurt, 22 men were in the dock. One of the defendants died before the trial actually got underway and another was relieved from prosecution for reasons of health. The other twenty who stood trial had been members of the SS. The principal defendant was Robert Mulka, the highest ranking of all the defendants. The accused came from all walks of life: about half of them were tradesmen or workers and four of them had an academic education.

The first phase of the trial consisted of the interrogation of the accused, which ended on February 6, 1964. Subsequently 248 witnesses were heard. An on-site inspection in Poland, with which West Germany did not yet have diplomatic relations, created a sensation. The prosecution and defense summations lasted three months, from early May to early August 1965. On August 19, the court pronounced the verdicts. Seventeen of the defendants received prison sentences (six life sentences, ten sentences ranged from three-and-one-half to fourteen years, and one was given juvenile custody for ten years because he was considered a juvenile at the time he committed his crimes). Three of the defendants were acquitted for lack of proof.

In contrast to the Eichmann trial, the judges at the Auschwitz trial had no interest in educating the public about the nature and extent of Nazi crimes; they were merely interested in determining the individual guilt or innocence of each of the defendants, based on the penal code (Naumann, 1965). One of the major issues brought up in the trial was the so-called "emergency orders" often cited by the defense. The court heard a number of prominent expert witnesses on this issue.

Public interest in the Auschwitz trial was relatively great, even if not as pronounced as during the Eichmann trial. No leading representatives of the Nazi regime stood before the court in Frankfurt as, for instance, in the Nuremberg trial and also no behind-the-scenes mastermind like Eichmann, who was intimately involved in the organization of the machinery of annihilation. On the contrary, the Auschwitz trial dealt with perpetrators who under "normal" conditions were unlikely to have committed the crimes attributed to them. None of them had committed criminal offenses after the war; most had established a "respectable middle-class" existence since then. In this trial the behavior of the "average" German was being questioned, which forced "the public to live with its past and become aware that not only the 'murderers' but also the 'accessories,' the supporters, the complacent, and the weak lived among the population" (Steinbach, 1984).

Although the Auschwitz trial was less spectacular than the Nuremberg trial, it also attracted considerable international attention. At the opening of the proceedings there were at least 120 to 150 representatives of the press, who again came from many lands, among them numerous Polish journalists. The proceedings ran their course under the floodlights of television and the flashbulbs of photojournalists. The site visit to Auschwitz in December 1964 took place in the presence of approximately 200 journalists.

As for other trials conducted in Germany, Grabitz (1988) claims that only the sensational ones were widely covered in Germany, such as those concerning events in the Auschwitz and Meidanek concentration camps and the trial of the Nazi criminal Kurt Lishka. Trials that had a local interest tended to be reported only on their first and last day. It is true, continues Grabitz, that there were some dedicated journalists who were committed to the subject and tried to report accurately about the background of those trials and their problems, but they had difficulties publishing their material. Editors restricted space in newspapers (as well as airtime), claiming that public interest in the trials was limited. Grabitz believed that this tendency would make it difficult for Germany to be able to preserve the memory of the Holocaust and prevent it from happening again.

THE DEMJANJUK TRIAL

Unusual conditions marked the trial of Ivan Demjanjuk, which took place in Jerusalem beginning in 1986 (Teicholz, 1990). Demjanjuk was thought to be the man who, because of his cruelty in the Treblinka concentration camp, was notoriously known as "Ivan the Terrible."

For more than twenty years John Demjanjuk had led an inconspicuous life in Cleveland, Ohio. He had emigrated to the United States with his wife in 1952. The couple had met in Germany in 1947 in a camp for so-called "displaced persons." After 1945 hundreds of thousands of people uprooted by the turmoil of war waited in such camps to find a new homeland somewhere. Demjanjuk had asserted to the international refugee organization of the United Nations that he had come to Germany as a prisoner of war. He gave his nationality as "Polish," although he actually came from the Ukraine. Years later it was ascertained that the information Demjanjuk provided about his nationality was as false as the answers to a number of other questions which the authorities had asked him.

To complete the required immigration application Demjanjuk had produced a passport photo. In the mid 1970s several Holocaust survivors believed that they recognized the person in the photograph as "Ivan the Terrible," who had supervised the operation of the gas chamber at the Treblinka concentration camp. The American Immigration and Naturalization Service began searching for Demjanjuk in 1975. A list of names of former Ukrainians who were accused of collaboration with the Nazis and who possibly lived in the United States had come before the authorities. The name Ivan Demjanjuk appeared on the list.

In the course of the investigation carried out in the United States and in Israel, the suspicion that the (since 1958) naturalized American had been directly involved in Nazi crimes was noticeably strengthened. Not only the survivors' statements claimed that Demjanjuk was "Ivan the Terrible." In the Soviet Union an identity card had turned up that identified Demjanjuk as an *SS*-guard trained in the Polish camp of Trawniki. The SS-guards there were recruited to work in concentration camps, especially from among the Ukrainians imprisoned there.

The momentum of suspicion against Demjanjuk was sufficient to begin deportation proceedings in the United States. To this end Demjanjuk's American citizenship was revoked. In 1983 Israel entered a request for extradition, which was granted three years later. Two days after the decision was reached Demjanjuk landed in Tel Aviv aboard an El Al airplane.

The preparations for Demjanjuk's trial lasted a whole year. Although the proceedings officially opened on November 26, 1986, the actual trial didn't begin until February 17, 1987. Demjanjuk's American and Israeli lawyers had one primary goal: to prove that the case was one of a mistaken identity and that their client was not the man known as "Ivan the Terrible." But the court gave more weight to the survivors of

Treblinka, who identified Demjanjuk as their tormentor, than to the defendant, who often contradicted himself.

Another important piece of circumstantial evidence in the trial was Demjanjuk's SS-service identity card, made available by the Soviets. On the identity card, which had both a photo and a signature, the card owner's place of service was given as Sobibor (another camp), not Treblinka. Although the defense insisted that the KGB (the Soviet Secret Police) had falsified the Trawniki papers, the court accepted the identity card as evidence. Demjanjuk was sentenced to death by hanging on April 18, 1988. Even after the verdict the condemned man continued to protest his innocence.

In fact, Demjanjuk's identity remained contested among the trial's observers (Wagenaar, 1988). Witnesses in earlier Nazi trials had unanimously testified that a man named Martschenko, not Demjanjuk, had borne the sobriquet of "Ivan the Terrible." However, attempts to ascertain Martschenko's whereabouts were unsuccessful. In this connection it seemed relevant to the court that Martschenko was the maiden name of Demjanjuk's mother.

The question also remained unanswered as to why Sobibor was given as Demjanjuk's place of service on the identity card, although witnesses claimed to have seen him in Treblinka. In its sentencing arguments the court held it to be entirely possible that Demjanjuk traveled back and forth between both camps without this being noted on his identity card.

Demjanjuk's lawyers lodged an appeal against the sentence with Israel's Supreme Court. More than two years after the end of the trial, in mid-May 1990, hearings in the appeals process began which lasted a total of seven weeks. In the subsequent examination by the Supreme Court new documents from the KGB archives were made available. After lengthy deliberations by the five justices, the death sentence was unanimously overturned and Demjanjuk was freed for lack of proof. The rationale for this decision was the not-to-be-dispelled doubt about the defendant's identity. Indeed, it had been proven that Demjanjuk had served in concentration camps, especially in Sobibor. However, the court was of the opinion that it was not in the position of pronouncing judgment on this, as he was formally charged and tried with being in Treblinka.

The trial took place in an auditorium usually used as a movie theater. Newspaper reporters occupied several rows of seats. Photographers and radio reporters, usually excluded from Israeli courtrooms, were admitted this time. As in the case of the Eichmann trial, by means of organized groups of high school students and soldiers attending court sessions Israel again sought to stimulate broad public interest in the Holocaust, especially among its young citizens. For this and other reasons, several critical Israeli observers, including Segev (1993), spoke of a show trial, albeit a fair one, and Demjanjuk's Israeli attorney, Yoram Sheftel, made numerous accusations along these lines following the trial.

In his book, *The Demjanjuk Affair: The Rise and Fall of a Show-Trial*, Sheftel (1994) referred to the trial as a "shameful show trial" (p. 10) and defined the functioning of the media as "delinquent and rowdy" (p. 301). The evidence he presents to support his claims deal both with the style and the judicial content. He describes the opening of the trial as a circus (p. 45) and compares the beginning of Demjanjuk's interrogation to the Academy Awards Ceremony:

"I thought to myself that the courtroom atmosphere was not appropriate for a trial of a man accused of murdering nine hundred thousand Jews but rather the preparation for the entrance of the movie stars to the hall where the Academy Awards Ceremony is held. Everybody was waiting for the appearance of Demjanjuk, the superstar" (p. 142). The audience's applause following the reading the verdict was, as far as Sheftel was concerned, a fitting ending of the "show" (p. 214).

However, not only the style of the trial bolsters Sheftel's argument. Even the judicial procedures signified "the loss of all criteria for a fair trial" (p. 214). The request by the defense to compel the prosecution to concentrate on bringing only those witnesses who could prove Demjanjuk's identity as "Ivan the Terrible" was denied. The prosecution was permitted to bring as many witnesses as it saw fit, even to prove facts concerning the Holocaust that the defense had not disputed. Hamerman (1986) claims that in the trial several forces were put in juxtaposition: hatred, vengeance, cruelty, and a curious passionate attraction to evil, whereas true pain and sorrow were pushed aside to some extent. Attention was diverted from the true nature of the historical phenomenon and concentrated on unimportant details, which fed feelings, passion, and human curiosity.

The acquittal in Israel's longest legal proceedings sparked differing reactions: disappointment and bitterness among Holocaust survivors versus satisfaction from many observers over the trial's adherence to the rule of law. At first Demjanjuk remained in Israeli protective custody while new applications for proceedings against him were submitted but rejected. In addition, there was a question as to which country would be willing to take him in. After initial resistance the United States announced that it was prepared to allow him to return. He was deported back to the United States in September 1993, after being in an Israeli prison for approximately eight years.

3

The Holocaust and the Israeli and German Societies

In order to understand the context, setting and circumstances of the trials, it is necessary to briefly discuss the social climate in Germany and Israel during the years following the Second World War vis-à-vis the Holocaust.

THE HOLOCAUST AND GERMAN SOCIETY

The Holocaust in German society has been a delicate subject and has gone through several stages since 1945 (Bier, 1986). These stages were, of course, different from those in Israel although the initial one, immediately following the war, was quite similar. It has repeatedly been claimed that Germans living in the Federal Republic of Germany (West Germany) made attempts to repress the Nazi past (Mitscherlich & Mitscherlich, 1991). The dominant idea of postwar Germany was that the Nazis were not true Germans but rather demonic intruders who came in at a certain point and threw Germany off its historical course. By disinheriting their Nazi past and opening a new leaf, starting afresh from zero hour (*Stunde Null*) the Germans could look at the future with a clear conscience (Klein, 1987). Accordingly, they were studiously forward looking, reluctant to confront the past (Marcuse, 1987). Kampe

(1987) refers to it as a "collective silence" with respect to recent history; a "clean sweep mentality" or "clean break" as Bergmann and Erb (1990) put it. This was all part of the German attempt to come to terms with the past, or as Renn (1987) refers to it, as "mastering the past"

Many Germans were disinclined to take part in the process of denazification; that is, removing former Nazis from all official positions. What made it even more difficult for the Germans was the fact that the British were not prepared to allow them a free hand in running what was supposed to be their own procedure. According to Marshall (1980), it seems that in retrospect the lack of spontaneous "settling of accounts" with the Nazis was one of the greatest mistakes of the Military Government. Support of a general denazification program was exhibited by only one quarter of the population. The active Nazis were not alone in rejecting what they considered intolerable Allied hypocrisy and pretense of moral superiority. There was widespread bitterness and a feeling that the denazification process was too rigid, too schematic, and went on for too long.

On the other hand, Marshall (1980) goes on to suggest, there were also Germans for whom the denazification was disappointing because it did not go far enough. These Germans were truly horrified by the evidence revealed after the war. Many criticized the Allies for not making a distinction between "good" and "bad" Germans. However, when it came to the feeling of guilt and responsibility for the crimes committed, there was widespread indifference. Most people wanted to forget or claimed ignorance about what had happened. Moreover, they maintained that given similar circumstances, this could happen anywhere.

When considering public opinion in Germany immediately following the war it is important to bear in mind that one of the aims of the Allied occupying forces was not only to make the Nazi government judicially accountable for its criminal actions but to re-educate the German population. To this end the American Office of Military Government (OMGUS) set up its own public opinion department. Through September 1949 this department conducted a large number of population surveys in the American occupied zone.

Between November 1945 and August 1946 many surveys were conducted to measure the German attitudes regarding the Nuremberg trial. Of course one must take into consideration the fact that the surveys were conducted by the occupiers and that therefore at least some of the respondents may have replied to questions in a manner suiting what they thought the interviewers wanted to hear.

A total of 2,969 people were polled. As it turned out, within a few weeks about two-thirds of the Germans had heard something about the trial. Later the percentage of the informed population rose to 87%. In responding to the question of what they had learned from the reporting, 29% initially said that the trial gave them an opportunity to learn about the concentration camps for the first time. By the second survey the corresponding figure had risen to 57%. Also, just less than one-third of those questioned reported that only during the trial did they hear anything about the annihilation of the Jews. An average of 80% believed that the war criminals received a fair trial, although the proportion of people who rendered this opinion decreased over time. A majority of the population was of the opinion that the defendants were guilty, and 70% believed that there were other guilty parties in addition to those on trial at Nuremberg. The surveys also showed that the majority of newspaper readers considered the newspaper reports of the trial to be thorough and credible.

By the end of February 1946 there was a decrease in interest in the trial proceedings, a tendency that continued for several months (Merritt & Merritt, 1970). Interest in the trial increased again in August, close to its conclusion. After the guilty verdicts were announced, public interest was almost as great as when the trial started. An overwhelming majority (93%) of the population said that they had heard about the verdicts. Most people said that they were satisfied with the thoroughness and credibility of the newspaper reports. The articles were more likely to be criticized, if at all, for being incomplete rather than for being imprecise.

Almost all of the people polled in the American zone (92%) rejected the idea of collective guilt. After the verdicts were handed down, 30% felt that what they had learned from the trial were the dangers of a dictator and one-sided politics, and one fourth of the respondents mentioned the importance of the maintenance of peace. Only very few (6%) voiced negative opinions, such as that there was no justice because only Germans were punished, or that politics should be avoided. Two-thirds gave no clear answer to this question. Every second person claimed to have become more aware of the atrocities in the concentration camps.

To the extent that these surveys can be considered valid, the data indicate that the Nuremberg trial and the newspaper reports about it were perceived by the German public as enlightening. Throughout the trial and its coverage, both on radio, which probably had a greater impact because it could reach more people, and in the press, the circulation of which was restricted due to a shortage of newsprint, the population could acquire information that until then was claimed to be unknown. The extent to which the German public did or did not know about the atrocities being committed while they were happening is a different issue that is beyond the present discussion. In short, what emerges from the data is that right after the war Germans seem to have been interested in the trial of Nazi war criminals, and that their attitudes concerning the reporting of the trial were positive, while at the same time there was widespread denial of their knowledge of the atrocities while they were taking place.

The attitude toward the Nazi trials evidently changed during the early 1950s. New surveys conducted by the Americans under the umbrella of the U.S. High Commission for Germany (HICOG) in the "semi-sovereign" Bundesrepublik after the Germans won the right for self-determination, showed three substantial trends. First, there was increasing disappointment with the justice exercised by the occupying powers in the Nuremberg and subsequent war crimes trials. There was a growing feeling that the trials were unfair (from 6% in October 1946 to 30% four years later) and that the verdicts were too harsh (from 9% to 40%). In addition, the waiver of charges against Allied war criminals was felt to be unjust. Second, more and more people felt that the time had come to put an end to the trials dealing with wartime actions. In the middle of 1952 only 10% of a national random sample of Germans agreed with the measures taken by the Allies with regard to war criminals, whereas six times as many (59%) disapproved of them. At the same time, a third sentiment was on the increase; namely, that the goal of the first trial was not actually to bring the criminals to justice, but that there was a political element involved. Thus, when the Allies commuted some sentences during the early 1950s, more than a few Germans saw this as a purely opportunistic attempt to draw former enemies into their own camp (Brochhagen, 1994).

Thus, by the time the Eichmann trial was being conducted in 1960-61, there was a different climate of opinion in Germany compared with what had been the situation in 1945-46. Although it is true that much attention was devoted in the German media to the trial, that German newspapers sent correspondents to Jerusalem, that in June 1960—even before the beginning of the trial—nine-tenths of the citizens of West Germany had heard of Eichmann's arrest (Institut für Demoskopie Allensbach, 1960), nevertheless only 14% of the population agreed that Eichmann should stand trial before an Israeli court (27% argued for an international tribunal and 25% felt that he should be put on trial in Germany). Also, a considerable portion of the public felt that Eichmann's abduction was unjustified. Only one-fifth of those polled conceded Israel the right to capture Eichmann by any means whatsoever.

Later, in June 1961, just a handful (4%) of those polled by the Institut für Demoskopie Allensbach (1961) admitted to not having heard of the Eichmann trial. Only 14% said that they didn't follow the trial, although it is quiet clear that most people read the reports only occasionally. The main sources of information about the trial were newspapers, followed by television; radio was in third place. However, despite the broad following, readiness to accept information and consternation about what was learned were quite limited. People were more interested in new twists in the trial and less concerned with the ongoing proceedings. When the surveys posed a concrete question, only a minority of respondents could give exact information. Indications of a collective feeling of guilt towards Jews or a pointed condemnation of anti-Semitic actions during the Third Reich were missing. Finally, critical views of the trial (e.g., that the death sentence Eichmann received was unjust) tended to increase after the trial.

The message being conveyed in Germany was that Germany today was different from Germany of the past and that Hitler and Eichmann should not be seen as synonymous with Germany. After admitting Eichmann's guilt and regarding it as part of the machinery of annihilation, the press went on to deal with the question of "German guilt." The main conclusion was that there was indeed a collective shame but not a collective guilt (Carmichael, 1961). The press had a less committed attitude, however, than that expressed by Theodor Heuss, West Germany's first president after the war, who declared that there is a collective German shame as well as collective responsibility and that Nazi war crimes trials are part of the attempt to deal with this responsibility (Grabitz, 1988). The newspapers referred to the helplessness of the Jews and generalized this to Germans as well, who could not resist the Nazis. The press also highlighted stories of rescue in which Germans saved Jews during the war (Carmichael, 1961).

Ariel (1961), who studied the neo-Nazi press, albeit quite limited, found that those newspapers tended to minimize the importance of the Eichmann trial. They contested the legality of the procedures and therefore opposed in advance any verdict that might be given. They claimed that the Holocaust as portrayed in the trial was highly exaggerated and that the figure of six million murdered Jews is imaginary. They also stressed the guilt of the Allies, whom they felt shared the responsibility by not bombing the death camps and the railroads leading to them.

There are indications that the Auschwitz trial drew less attention than did the Eichmann trial. In a survey administered by the DIVO Institute in June 1964, half a year following the commencement of the trial, three-fifths of the population knew about the trial but four out of ten people who had heard about it said that after so many years people shouldn't keep stirring up things that happened in Auschwitz (Schmidt & Becker, 1967). It seems that there was a growing proportion of people who were tired of dealing with the past. On the other hand, some scholars (e.g., Steinbach, 1981) consider the Auschwitz trial as a turning point. According to this view, the trial served as a first opportunity in the Federal Republic to examine the Nazi era and the mass murder of the Jews.

Although there is no doubt that both the Eichmann and Auschwitz trials brought the Holocaust back to German public awareness, the subject was treated with caution, for fear of arousing resentment in the general population. For example, Marcuse (1987) examined Holocaust memorials in Germany, which were quite rare in the 1960s, and which did not make any reference in their respective inscriptions to the atrocities committed during the Holocaust.

A discussion of these issues intensified once again in the late 1970s with regard to the controversy about the statute of limitations for Nazi crimes, which arose in the general context of statute of limitations for murder. Some members of the Bundestag (West German parliament) called for an end to any further prosecution of Nazi war criminals. This strong political desire on the part of the Federal Republic to unburden itself of its anti-Semitic past became quiet evident. The German public wanted to restore its self-esteem and to promote current German interests. Moreover, on the one hand, public airing of the issue of anti-Semitism was taboo, but on the other hand, several scandals in Germany brought the topic to the public agenda (Renn, 1987).

From the end of the 1970s a new process was taking place: the return of history into public awareness. Many had been searching for the historic roots of the German present and ultimately their own place in the history of the world. This trend culminated in the mid 1980s in what became known as the "historians' debate" (Baldwin, 1990; Maier, 1988), which Kampe (1987) described as an "intellectual civil war." The debate took place at first in two leading German newspapers, *Die Zeit* and the *Frankfurter Allgemeine Zeitung*, but soon included almost the entire media in West Germany. For the first time since the end of World War II, well-known German historians (e.g., Nolte, Hillgruber, and others) called for a new relationship with the past: to dissociate the Germans from the Nazi era and especially from the Holocaust. They went against the apologetic tendencies, as they called it, of contemporary German historiography. These new "revisionists" did not deny that the Holocaust occurred. Their objective was to explain the Holocaust in its historical context and with the aid of comparative historical analyses make it appear "normal," the result being that they trivialized it (Kampe, 1987).

Those who disagreed with this notion (represented by other prominent historians, such as Mommsen and Hildebrand) were against the comparisons being drawn between the Nazi regime and the Bolsheviks, or the Armenian massacre and the extermination of the Jews.

They claimed that justifying Nazi policies of violence by such comparisons was totally inappropriate. Without going into the specific arguments and counterarguments, what is clear is that there was wide public interest in history, evidenced also by the success of the Prussian Exhibition of 1981 in Berlin and the best-seller status of various historical monographs. No more "people without history": historical consciousness had once again become a factor of political orientation (Kampe, 1987).

In addition, during that period there were various events that brought the Holocaust to the public agenda. These include the televising of the mini-series *Holocaust*, which was broadcast in 1979, and the visit in 1985 of President Reagan to the German cemetery at Bitburg, which compelled the German political leadership to engage in public discussion of the Holocaust.

In 1986, the year the Demjanjuk trial began in Jerusalem, two-thirds of the German public spoke up for making a clean break with the Nazi past (Institut für Demoskopie Allensbach, 1986). Even so, three-fifths still stated that in recent years or even earlier they had read reports about the persecution of Jews during the Third Reich either very carefully (17%) or quite carefully (42%). Hence the wish to cut ties with the past had an informative basis. People knew about the past but wanted to have no connection with it. It seems that the notion of *Stunde Null*, which characterized the period immediately after the war, became in the 1980s once again a common sentiment with the German public. Thus, for example, when Bavarian Television decided in April 1986 to broadcast Claude Lanzmann's film *Shoah*, it was scheduled to be aired on Sunday mornings, a time when only few viewers were likely to watch it. The argument for selecting that time slot was that the public was satiated with the theme of the Holocaust (Renn, 1987). Likewise, more and more historians began to portray the Nazis as victims and there was a desire to identify with the soldiers who tried to defend their country, especially against Russia (Klein, 1987).

However, it seems that the picture of the social climate concerning this issue was more complicated. It is true that there was, on the one hand, the "clean sweep mentality" (Kampe, 1987), to which one might add the opposition to conducting more war crimes trials. Many felt that there was no longer any social purpose for punishment as the perpetrators had long been socially integrated (Grabitz, 1988). On the other hand, there were those who were committed to reconciling the tensions between Germans and Jews and who sincerely felt collective shame (Renn, 1987). Appropriately, just at that time the Commission Against Anti-Semitism was formed in West Berlin. This was the first time that West Germany had shown a commitment to monitor contemporary manifestations of anti-Semitism (Klein, 1987).

THE HOLOCAUST AND ISRAELI SOCIETY

In Israeli society, the Holocaust has a position of a "civil religion" and according to Liebman and Don-Yehia (1983) it serves as a central politi-cal myth, a symbol of Israel's position today and a legitimization for the Jewish claim to the land. The commemoration of the Holocaust includes certain rituals (e.g., standing for a moment of silence on Holocaust Memorial Day) and it even has its own shrine, *Yad Vashem*, where one is expected to behave like in any other holy place. Wolffsohn (1993), in dis-cussing the great importance of *Yad Vashem*, claims that it is the most important secular shrine and regards it as second in national reverence only to the Wailing (Western) Wall of the Temple Mount in Jerusalem.

According to Young (1993), who studied memorial sites in Israel and other countries, the commemoration of the Holocaust in Israel is manifested in daily experience. The strength that sustained the Jews and enabled them to survive the Holocaust sustains them still in their daily struggle in Israel. The memory of the Holocaust strengthens the connec-tion between its heroes and the Jews in Israel, and the victims of the Holocaust are considered part of those who died in defense of the coun-try. This is also evident in several museums for the Holocaust where the main images of that period are of heroism and opposition to the Nazis. What is significant is not the unprecedented destruction but the unprecedented heroism of those who rebelled in the ghettos.

Zionist ideology has made two demands on the Israeli people: on the one hand, to uproot the Holocaust from their daily lives in order to turn a "new leaf," and on the other hand, to keep the memory of the Holocaust alive in order to reify the turning of the leaf. Therefore, there is a constant need to nourish the memory of the Holocaust without allowing it to penetrate too much into the self-determination of the new collective (Zuckermann, 1993).

Empirical studies support the notion of the centrality of the Holocaust for Israeli society. Katz (1973) concluded that the Holocaust is high on peoples' minds and that they read much on the topic. This ten-dency was reconfirmed in a more recent study (Katz, Haas, Gurevitch, Weitz, Adoni, & Goldberg, 1992) which indicated consensus across vari-ous social strata on the centrality of Holocaust Memorial Day. Herman (1977) even argued that a true understanding of current Jewish identity is not possible without considering the deep, long-lasting effect that the memory of the Holocaust has had on its formation. In addition, various events such as acts of terror are often framed in the context of the Holocaust (Nossek, 1994).

Attitudes towards the Holocaust have changed over time. Following World War II and during the first years of the State, there was a tendency to play down the memory of the Holocaust. The events appeared to be so incredible that the public found them unbelievable (Bauer & Lowe, 1981; Zimmermann, 1994). Most of the information came from ideologically motivated survivors who had come to Palestine immediately following the war, including many of the leaders of the ghetto uprisings. The truth, as they saw and expressed it in central forums of the Jewish settlement of those days, contributed to the creation of the stereotypes of the time. It should be noted that 1945-1949 were the peak years in the diplomatic and military struggle for the State of Israel. Out of it emerged the myth of the new Israeli: self-confident, brave, strong, and successful. The values most appreciated were pioneering, tilling the soil, socialism, and focusing on the best interest of the collective, all of which were in contradiction to the characteristics of the Diaspora Jew—engaging in nonproductive occupations and showing signs of weakness and emotionalism. The Jews in Israel were no longer to be a humiliated and haunted minority but proud fighters. Those exterminated during the Holocaust became a symbol of the passiveness of the Diaspora that was now to be shrugged off. However, there were also the traumatic memories of the survivors who wanted to build new lives and there were guilt feelings among part of the local population who felt that they did not do enough to save their brethren. In many cases, these groups were actually close relatives, because the population in Palestine in those days was mostly of European origin. The first reaction of both segments of the population was deep mourning, which became the source for guilt feelings and repression. In addition, shame and humiliation was felt for what was perceived by the locals as the shameful behavior of European Jewry (Liebman & Don Yehia, 1983; Yablonka, 1994). The conspiracy of silence was accompanied by judgments and accusations directed towards the survivors who "went like sheep to the slaughter" (Bar-On, 1994; Porat, 1986). This was the atmosphere during the Nuremberg trial that can best be described as detachment from the Holocaust (Klein, 1987). The sole link to the Holocaust was through stories of heroism such as the story of the uprising of the Warsaw Ghetto.

Awareness of the Holocaust in the 1950s was low and it was seldom mentioned except for the public debate as to whether survivors and the State of Israel should accept reparations from Germany and the events surrounding the Kastner trial (a Jew accused of collaboration with the Nazis). During that period, no research was conducted on the subject except for some data collection at the *Beit Lochamey Hageta'ot* (Ghetto Fighters House) and beginning in 1953 at *Yad Vashem*. The approach to the subject was highly subjective and emotional and provoked wartime stereotypes of the Jews: on the one hand, the collaborators (the *Judenrats*), and on the other hand, the rebellious partisan heroes. In the middle were the masses that were led like "sheep to slaughter."

The problem accompanying Israel during its first years of statehood—absorbing new immigrants, establishing social and legal infrastructures, developing an economy, and securing the country's borders—were all of top priority and did not leave much time and energy to deal with traumas of the past (Bauer, 1990; Keren, 1985). This was the existence into which the survivors were drawn. Klein (1987) speaks in this context of the dilemma of the survivors' identity. They were eager to be like the local Israeli fighter but also felt great shame. That was the time when the term "shameful secret" was coined. This common secret was shared by the newly arrived survivors, the veteran Israelis, and the national leadership, including Prime Minister David Ben-Gurion, who was admired by all. Since national mourning did not begin immediately following the Holocaust, it became something shameful, secretive, and private.

At a meeting in New York in March 1960 between Ben-Gurion and the German Chancellor, Konrad Adenauer, the question of establishing diplomatic relations between Israel and Germany was discussed and naturally made headlines (Prittie, 1967). The Eichmann trial, which was taking place at that time, added another angle to the complex triangle: Israelis, Germans, and the Holocaust.

The trial was perceived by many (e.g., Hausner, 1968; Herman, 1977; Robinson, 1965) as a turning point in relating to the Holocaust. For the first time the Holocaust became the focus of national attention. The headline "Tense Anticipation for the Opening of the Holocaust Trial," which appeared in Israel's *Yedioth Aharonoth* on April 10, 1961, demonstrates that Eichmann was considered a representative of the Holocaust itself. The trial was meant to express historical justice accompanied by a "statement" that the Jewish people had survived despite everything that had happened (Zuckermann, 1993). The editorial in *Ha'aretz* on April 11, 1961 summarized it all in one sentence: "It is not only justice bestowed upon one man but justice for the history of an entire people."

The profound change was manifested not only in the unprecedented public interest in the trial but also in its attitude towards the Holocaust. For the first time there was an attempt to get closer to the survivors and understand them without the contempt and alienation that accompanied their image as "sheep going to slaughter." Before the Eichmann trial it was difficult to conceive of an editorial on that topic like the one that appeared in *Ha'aretz* on April 4, 1961. It raised the question of whether the young generation, being strong, tanned, and willing to fight could be able to understand their pale, submissive fathers. Could they understand that this compliant, obedient generation, in spite of the death of six million Jews, fulfilled its primary duty to stay alive as a people in unprecedented, difficult conditions? The attempt to bring the young generation closer to the Holocaust and explain what happened was indeed one of the declared aims of the trial. The young generation was exposed to details it had not known before. The trial served as an opportunity to teach youngsters about the atrocities committed during the Second World War (Keren, 1985).

Based on research conducted among populations differing in their involvement with the trial, Herman, Peres, and Yuchtman (1965) concluded that the impact of the Eichmann trial was profound on all groups. Publishers who had thus far refrained from releasing books on the Holocaust for fear that they would not sell began to print more and more memorial volumes. Also, the testimony and the great number of documents presented at the trial served as an impetus for research (Keren, 1985). A study conducted in Israel about the effect of the Eichmann trial on young citizens (Deutsch, 1974) showed that two-fifths of those questioned had read relevant literature about the Holocaust before or during the trial, and 10% did so after the trial.

The Eichmann trial took place in a period in which heroism was strongly related to the perception of the Holocaust. However, along with that a more open attitude developed towards the survivors who were not "heroes," having "merely" survived. Until the Eichmann trial, those who were saved by luck more than by active resistance did not get any public attention (Young, 1993).

The dramatic changes in the emotional attitude towards the survivors must be viewed in light of the changes that the Israeli society underwent during the early days of the new State. National reconciliation and the international position of Israel were strengthened. However, there were still serious problems that the Israeli revolution did not solve: the future of the country was not yet assured; most of the Jews were still in the Diaspora; the withdrawal from the Sinai, which was done under joint U.S.-Soviet pressure following the joint British-French-Israeli operation against Egypt in October 1956, was still seen as shameful submission; and along with increased individualism the pioneering spirit began to wane. The Eichmann trial was thus supposed to remind the people that only the State of Israel could ensure security of the Jews. In addition there was a great need to coalesce among Ashkenazi and Sephardic Jews, especially following the violent 1959 riot between them in the Haifa neighborhood of Wadi Salib. A cathartic patriotic experience such as the Eichmann trial was just the right thing at the right time. It also proved that in spite of the reparations agreement and an arms deal with Germany, the Ben-Gurion government was not indifferent to the memory of the Holocaust (Segev, 1993).

Not long after the Eichmann trial, in 1963, a report surfaced concerning German scientists helping Egypt develop weapons that could be
used against Israel. This served as another opportunity to discuss the
Holocaust in the context of Germans siding with Israel's enemies in
order to exterminate the Jews. This took place at the time of the
Auschwitz trial while the atrocities committed there became headlines
once again.

The Six-Day War in June 1967, and especially the anxious period
immediately preceding it, once again brought widespread feelings of
animosity from the entire world and the realization that the Israeli army
was the only guarantee for the Holocaust not to happen again (Keren,
1985). The direct threat of extermination in the weeks preceding the war
rekindled the images of the Holocaust (Herman, 1977). The Israeli press
often associated President Nasser of Egypt with Hitler and compared
the suggestions for settling the dispute by diplomatic means to the surrender agreement that was forced upon Czechoslovakia in World War II
(Segev, 1993). The persistence, sense of independence, and reliance on
Israel's own power were not compatible with the Diaspora spirit. But
after the war, one could detect once more a greater tolerance for the
Diaspora. The Six-Day War instigated a legitimacy crisis with regard to
the territories occupied during the war. The solution according to
Liebman and Don-Yehia (1983) was to turn to Jewish tradition as a basis
for legitimizing the State of Israel. Becoming more open to tradition
facilitated a more open attitude towards the Jewish experience in the
Diaspora, including the Holocaust.

During the time between the Six-Day War and the Yom Kippur
War (in 1973) there was a decline in public awareness of the Holocaust.
The Israeli public was preoccupied with daily troubles: the war of attri-
tion along the Suez Canal (that ended in Summer 1970) as well as other
security problems and the deterioration of Israel's foreign relations. The
Holocaust was mentioned from time to time only on special occasions
such as a visit of German dignitaries to Israel and an Israeli sports
team's refusal to visit Dachau in 1972 (Keren, 1985).

The Yom Kippur War instigated fear and heavy existential questions going back to the Holocaust period. The isolation of Israel, the sev-
erance of diplomatic relations by several countries, the refusal of other
countries to allow passage of arms to Israel—all these recalled the attitude of the world towards the Jews at the time of the Holocaust
(Herman, 1977). The airing of the television series *Holocaust* in 1978
added a sociocultural angle to the reactions towards the tragedy. The
myth of the independent Sabra (native-born Israeli), the hero and win-
ner, was shattered and made room for greater acceptance of Diaspora
Jews and their experience. The new civil religion, therefore, paid more

respect to the Jewish experience in the Diaspora, including the Holocaust (Liebman & Don-Yehia, 1983).

Despite all these developments, the Ministry of Education showed no interest in systematically teaching about the Holocaust until the late 1970s. Only in 1980 did the Knesset amend the Public Education Law, thereby mandating the teaching about the Holocaust in Israel's school system.

In the 1970s the historical dimensions of the Holocaust began to emerge. In this sense, first-hand experience of the survivors became an "historical experience" and an historical context for their testimonies was created (Bauer & Lowe, 1981). Moreover, Bauer (1990) speaks of the socialization of the issue. Whereas in the 1960s and early 1970s one would often hear from Sephardic Jews that the Holocaust was an Ashkenazi affair, in the 1980s these differences had become blurred. Youngsters from all origins had been going on trips to visit the death camps in Poland and had attended university courses on the topic, thereby indicating continued interest in the subject. The research by Bar-On and Sela (1991) supports the notion that the Holocaust had become an issue of common concern to all Israelis above and beyond differences of origin and culture. The work by Farago (1984) also supports this by showing wide consensus and interest concerning the Holocaust. Feelings towards immigrants, particularly those from Russia, also stemmed from the Holocaust, especially with regard to the perception that the Israelis were rescuing the newcomers from persecution and pogroms. The same was true regarding attempts to bring Jews from Iran, Syria, and Argentina (Bauer, 1990).

Former Prime Minister Menachem Begin had an important role in placing the Holocaust on the public agenda. According to Segev (1993), Begin more than anyone else popularized the Holocaust. Begin would compare the Covenant of the PLO (the Palestine Liberation Organization) to Hitler's *Mein Kampf* and used to mention the Holocaust on numerous occasions, such as when Israel bombed Iraq's nuclear reactor in June 1981. He justified the attack by the argument that it was going to prevent another Holocaust. This trend of popularization continued, for example, with a live broadcast of the "Heroism Quiz" from Auschwitz and the appearance of a Hebrew version of the American comic book *Maus*.

This was the background for the Demjanjuk trial. Caspi (1988) claims that the Demjanjuk trial accelerated painful processes of banalization and vulgarization of the Holocaust, falling prey to the political polarization of right and left in Israel. He argues that during the Demjanjuk trial the functioning of the media became a controversial issue. There were those who claimed that the media convicted the defendant before giving him a chance for a fair trial. There were journalists who expressed doubts as to the identity of the defendant or the justification of conducting the trial altogether. Some of the reports were biased and claims were made that the press contributed to the humanization of the defendant. Caspi attributed all this to the growing polarization between left and right in Israel. The left was convinced that the memory of the Holocaust, which strengthened nationalism and activism, was an obstacle to promoting "dovish" policies. The right also found itself facing a dilemma. On the one hand, the trial could aggravate the suspicion of strangers and strengthen the feeling that the "whole world is against us." On the other hand, adding a self-declared right-wing Israeli lawyer to the defense team was hard for the right to swallow. Finally, following the verdict the press was flooded by articles objecting to a death sentence.

Segev (1994b), too, believes that the social climate in Israel at the time of the Demjanjuk trial was important for understanding the way the press handled the subject. As noted, some members of the Israeli public had reservations about conducting the trial. There were those who saw it as a dangerous trap, especially if it would not be possible to prove Demjanjuk's guilt. The press expressed the various opinions and did not stick to one position, as was the case during the Eichmann trial. During the Demjanjuk trial there was great awareness that the Holocaust served political goals and this in turn caused cynicism in the press. The Holocaust was deeply rooted in Israeli society and most people knew more than they could have learned from the trial. This facilitated a more direct, less emotional approach to the legal procedures, especially as much of the testimony was of a technical and scientific nature.

Bar-On and Sela (1991) also speak about the "mobilization" of the Holocaust by the right, which claimed that Israelis must be strong because of what happened during the Holocaust, and by the left, which believed that because of the Holocaust Israel must make sure not to do to others what others did to its people.

Further evidence of the dominance of and the openness towards the Holocaust is found in the personal identification that many Israelis were feeling (Levy, 1985). One such expression of identification with the Holocaust was the maintenance of less judgmental attitudes towards the survivors. For example, students who participated on a trip to Poland also claimed that they were unable to judge the survivors and therefore could not regard those who were exterminated as "sheep going to slaughter" (Asa & Dgani, 1991). The increased openness to the subject and the need to provide testimony before they die strengthened in many survivors the desire to tell what happened to them during World War II (Bar-On, 1994).

It thus seems that attitudes towards the Holocaust underwent a process of normalization. It was no longer a sacred topic above criticism. Doubts were expressed in many circles concerning the wisdom of putting Demjanjuk on trial. The trips of youngsters to the death camps also began to stir public debate, thus reflecting the lifting of the taboo of discussing the commemoration of the Holocaust. Those opposing the trips expressed fear that they would instigate nationalistic sentiments, which might also bear on relations between Jews and Arabs. They preferred to add deeper and more comprehensive content to the memory of the Holocaust beyond mere ceremonies.

By combining the memory of the Holocaust with daily experiences there is greater harmony in the perception of what happened in the Holocaust and what is happening today. Not a different planet anymore, Auschwitz is now part of the past but with clear implications for the present and the future.

4

The Framework of
the Study

The goal of the present study was to examine the depiction of the Holocaust and the Nazi era by means of German and Israeli newspaper reporting about four Nazi trials. The study reported in this volume consists of a comprehensive and systematic quantitative content analysis of the press coverage of the four trials that were held in Germany and in Israel over the course of 43 years, from 1945 to 1988. The main focus of the study is on how the Holocaust was depicted in newspapers in the two countries as they reported on each of the trials.

One of the major advantages of doing research by means of content analysis is the ability to retrospectively study phenomena using products that were created by the people involved in the events. In fact, many historical topics can be studied using media sources, mainly newspapers, provided that the researchers are able to contextualize the materials and place them in a proper social and historical perspective.

Accordingly, content analytic studies are by definition one step removed from the events being depicted in the press. In the case of the Holocaust as it was unraveled in the course of the Nazi war crimes trials, however, the study is even further removed. As indicated earlier, the Holocaust was by and large not reported in real time by journalists; hence much of what appeared in the press came from trial proceedings, which journalists had better access to. And yet, even while the various trials were taking place during the past half century, with only minor exceptions focusing on one particular trial at a time (most notably the

Eichmann trial), no comprehensive longitudinal study was conducted on the overall coverage given to this subject by the media.

Every content analytic study involves making choices. The first set of choices in the current study was concerned with which comparative dimensions to use. Two dimensions were selected: country and time frame.

Whereas it is clear that all four trials were relevant to both Germans and Israelis, the location of the trials might have differentially weighed their salience and perceived importance. Thus, the trials that took place in Germany would naturally be more salient for the Germans and the trials conducted in Israel would be more important for Israelis. The design of the study, however, called for the analysis of press reports and editorial material concerning all four trials in both countries. This made it possible to examine how the press in each country dealt with each of the four trials and to probe the influence of the trial locations on the press coverage; that is, based on whether they were domestic or foreign events.

Even though the present study was conducted more than 40 years after the end of World War II, it attempted to provide a broad overview of an entire epoch in which Nazi war crimes trials were conducted. In fact, few historical studies using content analysis have spanned such a broad period. Moreover, most historical studies are not laden with the traumatic and emotional overtones that typify the Holocaust.

One must, however, keep in mind that the study deals with only a section of the judicial, political, and spiritual-moral examination of the Holocaust in both countries. Of course not all of the Nazi trials during the postwar years could be included in the study and it was also not possible to include other forms and ways in which the Nazi era was examined.

As noted earlier, there were also other occasions for dealing with the Holocaust and the Nazi era, including the creation of memorial days and debates over a possible statute of limitations for Nazi crimes, as well as the publication of books and the release of films about the persecution of Jews, and especially the "media event" created by the television series *Holocaust*. In this respect the reporting of the Nuremberg, Eichmann, Auschwitz, and Demjanjuk trials that were analyzed here are embedded in the long-term and more extensive process of "overcoming the past." And although it is difficult to isolate the role of these four trials from the entire process, it is surely justified to consider them as having had a profound impact; hence they were chosen to be at the center of the current study.

The fact that the four trials spanned a period of over 40 years has two main implications. First, the different amounts of time that had passed since the concrete events that were under scrutiny in the different courtrooms—all having taken place in the same period leading up to and during World War II—would conceivably affect the way the press approached the trials in general and the subject of the Holocaust in particular.

In addition to the elapsed time dimension, the nature and format of the press as well as the role of journalists, the techniques they use, the technology available to them, and the general media environment, have dramatically changed over the years. Without attempting to make any qualitative evaluation, several main phenomena must be noted: the size of newspapers has grown; the speed at which material is obtained has increased; editing techniques have become more sophisticated; and other media, notably television, have appeared on the scene and later dominated it. All these factors could have had an effect on how the trials were reported in the newspapers.

Finally, in both Germany and Israel, as in many other countries, different newspapers can be characterized as having certain political inclinations, ranging from left to right or liberal to conservative. The rationale for the selection of the particular newspapers included in the current study was to obtain as broad a range as possible of the press in both countries. Another consideration was to attempt to use newspapers that existed throughout the entire period under investigation; that is, to exclude newspapers that began to appear after the Nuremberg trial or ceased publication before the Demjanjuk trial. This was not entirely possible, however, thus necessitating some compromises, as will be detailed below.

THE NEWSPAPERS STUDIED

Shortly following World War II, the German press went through a major transition. The former newspapers, which had supported the Nazi regime, ceased publication and new newspapers began to appear, all having to be licensed by the Allied forces that controlled Germany, and published under their watchful eyes. Given the fact that quite a number of newspapers have appeared in the Federal Republic of Germany during the period of the study, significant selection was necessary.

In Germany, four daily newspapers were included in the analysis for each of the four trials: *Die Welt*, the *Frankfurter Allgemeine Zeitung*, the *Süddeutsche Zeitung*, and the *Frankfurter Rundschau*. These four publications are of high editorial quality and enjoy relatively large, albeit varied circulation. Moreover, the four newspapers represent "the entire political spectrum in the German daily press, from right, to moderate right, to moderate left, to left" (Wilke, 1994). And yet, it was also necessary to use two additional German dailies because *Die Welt* was first licensed when the Nuremberg trial was already underway and the *Frankfurter Allgemeine* first appeared three years after the Nuremberg trial. Therefore, these two newspapers could not be used for the analysis of the Nuremberg trial. In their place, for the Nuremberg trial only, the *Nürnberger Nachrichten* and the Berlin newspaper *Tagesspiegel* were substituted. The former was chosen because it was published in the city where the trials took place; the latter because it came from the capital of the former Reich, which since the German surrender in 1945 was under the control of the four occupying powers.

Regarding Israel, as was briefly noted earlier, the Nuremberg trial took place before the establishment of the State in May 1948. Nonetheless, even prior to the termination of the British mandate in Palestine, several Hebrew newspapers appeared. Most of these were highly political, representing either Zionist (socialist left or revisionist right) or religious viewpoints. Each newspaper served a particular segment of the politically divisive Jewish population, with information and editorial opinions custom-made for the respective groups. During the decades following national independence the circulation of the "independent" newspapers kept increasing while some of the political newspapers shut down.

For the current study a full range of newspapers was used. The following four newspapers were analyzed for all four trials: *Hatzofeh, Yedioth Aharonoth, Ha'aretz,* and *Davar*. In addition, *Hamashkif* was used for the Nuremberg trial and *Herut* was used for the Eichmann and Auschwitz trials. These newspapers could be said to represent the entire political spectrum in Israel (Caspi & Limor, 1999).

Whereas German newspapers regularly report on their circulation, Israeli newspapers have refrained from publishing such data on a regular basis, despite pressures to do so by the Israel Advertisers' Association (Caspi & Limor, 1999). Therefore, the data on circulation presented below can be considered valid in the German case, but only estimates, based on readership surveys and other sources, in the Israeli case.

Following is a brief description of the above-mentioned German and Israeli newspapers used in the study, presented in the chronological order in which they first appeared.

THE GERMAN NEWSPAPERS

Frankfurter Rundschau [Frankfurt Round View]

The first newspaper license granted by the American occupation forces in Germany was given to seven opponents of the Nazis, who set out to publish the *Frankfurter Rundschau* (Carlebach, 1985). Its first edition appeared on August 1, 1945, barely three months after the capitulation of the Third Reich. At first it appeared twice a week in a four-page edition, and by the end of October it had reached a circulation of over half a million.

After the repeal of the licensing requirement, the ownership of the *Frankfurter Rundschau* changed several times. At the time of the study, it was owned by the Karl Gerold Foundation, which guaranteed its independence. Although it is nationally available, its main distribution is in Frankfurt and the surrounding area. In comparison with other regional newspapers in Germany, it is well endowed.

According to Maassen (1986), the political orientation of the *Frankfurter Rundschau* has been considered as left to left-liberal. Above all, it became the organ of "progressive" circles during the course of the student movements of the 1960s. In its own words, the newspaper wants to "build a public that will monitor governments, administrations, the economy, law, etc." (p. 100).

Der Tagesspiegel (Berlin) [Berlin Daily Mirror]

The first independent daily newspaper in Berlin after the collapse of the Nazi regime appeared on September 27, 1945. In contrast to its otherwise customary practice, the American occupying forces dispensed with pre-censorship for the first six weeks of publication (Mendelssohn, 1959). Following the model of the *London Times*, *Tagesspiegel* began with three editions per week but as of November 1945 became a daily newspaper. The beginning circulation consisted of 200,000 copies. The interest in the newspaper in Berlin was great and in the beginning of 1946 the *Tagesspiegel* was the most widely read of Berlin's newspapers (Hurwitz, 1972).

The newspaper's upward trend did not last, however, mainly because it was a newspaper without a natural "hinterland." After reaching a peak in circulation of 450,000 copies, it declined rapidly as a result of the Berlin blockade. An additional obstacle was the Soviet ban on its sale in East Berlin and its zone border areas. The daily circulation of the Tagesspiegel fell from 315,000 to 100,000 before the start of the blockade.

During the time of the study, the nonprofit *Tagesspiegel Press Foundation* was in charge of guaranteeing the newspaper's independence. The board of trustees, composed of publishing and editorial staff members as well as shareholders, is responsible for the financial stability of the newspaper.

Süddeutsche Zeitung (Munich) [South German Newspaper]

The first license for the establishment of a newspaper in Bavaria was granted to a group of three journalists and two managing publishers. Their heirs have continuously run the newspaper ever since (Maassen, 1986). It is noteworthy that the first printing plate for the new newspaper used the melted-down lead type from Hitler's *Mein Kampf*. The first edition of the *Süddeutsche Zeitung* appeared on October 6, 1945 as the only newspaper in the area, with an initial circulation of 357,000 copies. At first it was published twice weekly and consisted of four and later six pages. Even though a second newspaper appeared in Munich in November 1946, which cost the *Süddeutsche Zeitung* a drop in circulation, it nevertheless remained the most widely read newspaper in the American zone, with a circulation of 255,000 copies, putting it at the top of the licensed newspapers in June 1949.

From its beginning the *Süddeutsche Zeitung* was primarily a local and regional newspaper. In the 1980s two-thirds of its copies were sold in Munich and its surroundings; therefore in a strict sense it cannot be considered a national newspaper. All the same, the national circulation is relatively high, higher than that of other regional subscription newspapers. At the time of the study, the *Süddeutsche Zeitung* was one of the largest circulating German dailies. In terms of its political inclination, the *Süddeutsche Zeitung* is situated left of center.

Nürnberger Nachrichten [The Nuremberg News]

The *Nürnberger Nachrichten*, the first German newspaper on the market in Nuremberg after World War II, was first published on October 11, 1945. In contrast to the usual licensing practice in the American zone, the licensing authority granted permission to establish a newspaper to an individual rather than to a committee of publishers. The license was awarded to the "independent-liberal" Joseph Ernst Drexel on the condition that he immediately seek a partner (Hurwitz, 1972).

Drexel had been repeatedly arrested during the Third Reich as an enemy of the Nazis and in July 1944 was deported to the Mauthausen concentration camp. At first he sought a partner for the newspaper among friends in the resistance movement. His "silent partner" was Hans Walter, a member of the former resistance movement in Nuremberg. However the Americans insisted that Drexel take in another partner as well. In January 1949 Heinrich G. Merkel, who did not belong to any political party, became a partner with 45% of the shares. Merkel was primarily responsible for the business side while Drexel was in charge of the editorial tasks.

From the beginning Drexel stressed the independence of his newspaper, which was demonstrated not only with regard to the American authorities, but also toward the German government. His opposition to Chancellor Adenauer's foreign policy in the postwar years established the reputation of the *Nürnberger Nachrichten* as a "left-liberal" newspaper.

The distribution allotted by the American licensors provided the *Nürnberger Nachrichten* a strong position in central Franconia, serving Nuremberg and its rural vicinity. After licensing was no longer required the circulation dropped due to the reestablishment of numerous local newspapers, but the existence of the *Nürnberger Nachrichten* was never in danger. On the contrary, its circulation increased over the following years and at the time of the current study it was the regional newspaper with the highest circulation.

Die Welt (Bonn/Hamburg) [The World]

Although *Die Welt* was established during the period when licensing was still required, it is not one of the so-called "licensed newspapers." Published at first under the aegis of the British, the authorities wanted it to function as a model for the licensed press in the British zone. The idea was that *Die Welt* should become a kind of German *Times* (Fischer, 1966).

The editorial staff of *Die Welt* consisted mainly of German journalists, with chief editor Rudolf Kustermeier at the helm, although control of the newspaper was in British hands. *Die Welt* did not become independent of the British until May 1950. The newspaper appeared in Hamburg on April 2, 1946 with an initial circulation of 160,000 copies. Due to a shortage of newsprint, it first appeared only twice a week. One year later, in June 1947, it began to appear three times a week with a circulation of 600,000 copies. Since the beginning of 1947 the newspaper was connected with the communications network of the London *Times*. The newspaper reached its highest circulation between July and September 1949 with a daily circulation of one million copies.

However the repeal of the licensing requirement in September 1949 and the ensuing swell in the number of new newspapers drastically reduced its circulation. Eventually the financially weakened newspaper went up for sale. In 1953 the publisher Axel Springer took over and named Hans Zehrer, who had once been turned down by the British, as editor-in-chief. Zehrer succeeded in attracting a number of notable journalists to *Die Welt*. However, in the 1960s, especially during the student movement, the newspaper's conservative-right orientation sparked controversy and several of its journalists resigned. At the time the current study was conducted, *Die Welt* saw itself as "independent of party and special interests, loyal to the state, open to reform from a conservative point of view" (Maassen, 1986).

Frankfurter Allgemeine Zeitung [Frankfurt General Newspaper]

As noted, the allied occupying powers repealed the licensing requirements in September 1949. Several weeks later, on November 1, 1949, the first edition of the *Frankfurter Allgemeine Zeitung* appeared (Dohrendorf, 1990). The driving journalistic force behind the establishment of the "newspaper for Germany," as its subtitle suggested, was Erich Welter, a former editor of the *Frankfurter Zeitung*, which was prohibited by the Nazis in 1943 (Gillessen, 1986). The *Frankfurter Allgemeine Zeitung* wanted to follow this tradition.

The *Frankfurter Allgemeine Zeitung* does not have an editor-in-chief. Its five editors have an equal say in all questions concerning individual departments. Their contract, drafted in December 1949, requires the newspaper to remain completely independent of government, party, and interest groups, in order to maintain a free and democratic civic foundation (Fischer, 1966). As of April 1959, a majority of the *Frankfurter Allgemeine Zeitung* is owned by the FAZIT-Foundation, whose objective is to guarantee the newspaper's independence.

The circulation began with 9,000 copies and grew rapidly. In 1982 its official circulation was quoted at 230,018 and in 1992 the *Frankfurter Allgemeine Zeitung* had the largest circulation of any nationally distributed subscription newspaper, with nearly 420,000 copies. The newspaper publishes a national as well as a regional edition.

THE ISRAELI NEWSPAPERS

Although several non-Hebrew newspapers have been published in Israel, most of the newspapers are in Hebrew; hence only the latter were used in the study. Also, as noted, some of these newspapers began to appear during the British mandate for Palestine, long before the State of

Israel was founded. All the newspapers described below are national newspapers. Some of them exist until today but others have folded at different points in time (Caspi, 1986; Caspi & Limor, 1999).

Ha'aretz [The Land]

Ha'aretz, the oldest Hebrew daily newspaper included in the current study, has the best reputation among Israeli newspapers. Ha'aretz originally evolved as part of a trilingual publication established in 1918 by the British military authority in Palestine (the other languages being English and Arabic). After World War I the newspaper was sold to Yehuda Leib Goldberg, a Russian Zionist, who moved its editorial offices to Jerusalem. In 1922 the newspaper was sold again to a group of Russian immigrants and in 1937 was sold for the last time, to its current owners, the Schoken family, publishers of German descent who had emigrated to Palestine. For technical reasons, the newspaper first appeared in the evening but later became a morning newspaper (Stock, 1954).

Ha'aretz was closely linked with the General Zionists Movement, which later became the Progressive Party. And yet, Ha'aretz is a politically independent liberal newspaper with an antisocialist position on economic and social matters and "dovish" antinationalist sentiments regarding security and foreign policy. Its elitist image can be attributed to its high journalistic standards as well as to its highly educated readership, many of whom serve in key political, economic and social positions. Whereas its pre-State circulation was around 11,000 copies, its current (estimated) circulation is at 50,000 copies, mostly by subscription; hence its reputation far exceeds its power based on its circulation.

Davar [The Issue]

The Histadrut, the Jewish labor federation, was founded in Palestine long before the State of Israel came into existence. Berl Katznelson, one of its leaders, established Davar in 1925. For many years Davar was closely associated with Mapai, one of Israel's socialist parties (the other socialist parties had their own newspapers). Davar was perceived as an important socializing agent for social and political values; thus many of its top editorial positions were party appointments and its contents closely fit the party ideology, including strict political censorship on many domestic matters.

During the pre-State years *Davar* as well as the other newspapers supported the national struggle, including free immigration to Palestine, settlement of the land, economic development, self-defense, and opposition to the British. During the 1950s there was no significant difference between party and independent newspapers in their attitudes towards the national leadership. In the 1970s, *Davar* became more critical of the government, a fact that was exemplified with the introduction of a weekly satirical supplement. Most of its circulation of about 21,000 during the 1980s was sold on a subscription basis.

The decline of the party press, which began in the 1960s, hit *Davar* as well. Its circulation gradually decreased and it began to suffer great financial losses, which the *Histadrut* could not absorb. In 1990 the subtitle "The Journal of the Laborers of Israel" was deleted in an attempt to attract a broader readership but without much success. In 1996 *Davar* folded after publishing nearly 22,000 editions.

Hamashkif [The Spectator]

During the years that it appeared, 1936-1949, *Hamashkif* was the official organ of the right-wing Revisionist Movement. Ever since the *Etzel* underground declared a rebellion against the British in early 1944, the newspaper was forced to maintain a delicate balance between the movement and the British authorities. *Hamashkif* was a legal newspaper even though most of its employees and readers were members of an illegal organization. The goal of the newspaper was similar to that of the underground movement, but its desire to keep publishing compelled it to compromise and moderate its messages. Nevertheless, the newspaper presented a tough nationalistic stance. In a 1941 article, *Hamashkif* clearly stated that it was not a newspaper in the purely journalistic sense but rather a platform for the dissemination of attitudes and feelings of the national movement and its members. Much of the space in *Hamashkif* was devoted to glorifying its leader, Zeev Jabotinsky, and considerable space was also devoted to advancing national Hebrew culture. Compared with other organs of the Revisionist Movement, *Hamashkif* survived for a relatively long time, but upon the termination of the British mandate for Palestine and the establishment of the State of Israel it folded and was succeeded by *Herut*, also published by former members of the underground.

Hatzofeh [The Observer]

Hatzofeh, the official newspaper of the National Religious Party, was founded by Rabbi Bar-Ilan, one of the leaders of the *Mizrachi* religious movement, which had commenced its activities in 1902. *Hatzofeh* first appeared in Jerusalem in 1937 three times a week, with a circulation of about 3,000 copies. Later that year it became a daily and its offices moved to Tel Aviv. The newspaper was initially considered a news source and vehicle for Jewish-national traditions. Most of its space was devoted to editorial and opinion articles expressing national-religious sentiments.

The paper's second editor, who was not a member of the *Mizrahi* movement, tried to change the character of the newspaper by making it more news-oriented at the partial expense of traditional Jewish material. There was much opposition to this change that brought about an official proclamation making the newspaper the official organ of the movement, whose tripartite bases were the Torah of Israel, the people of Israel, and the land of Israel. These three factors influenced the contents of the newspaper on a day-to-day basis.

When it was founded, *Hatzofeh* had a circulation of about 3,000 copies, mainly as subscriptions. In the late 1980s its circulation reached approximately 17,000 copies. In recent years it has been declining coincidentally with the decline in the political power of its sponsor, the National Religious Party.

Yedioth Aharonoth [The Late News]

Yedioth Aharonoth, the current leading newspaper in Israel in terms of circulation, first appeared in 1939, as a two-page newspaper, in two daily editions: one at noon and one in the evening, each with about 3,000 copies. As of 1940 it appeared only once a day, as an "evening" newspaper, late in the morning. Its founder was the Mozes family, whose descendants still own most of its stock. At the beginning of 1948, on the eve of national independence, *Yedioth Aharonoth* was a financially sound newspaper. However, in mid-February, nine years after its establishment, the newspaper suffered a serious crisis: many of its editorial and management staff abruptly quit their posts and founded a competing evening paper, *Ma'ariv*. The goal of the "dissidents" was to establish a newspaper under their full control in all areas, including its financial management. *Ma'ariv* became and remained the leading Israeli daily for the following two decades. In the mid-1970s, however, *Yedioth Aharonoth* began to recover. Its layout, easily understood language, and often sensational content addressed itself to a mass market, markedly raising its circulation.

Yedioth Aharonoth currently sells nearly 350,000 copies on weekdays and about 600,000 copies on weekends, and enjoys a readership of about two-thirds of the entire population of the country. It is published in tabloid form with bold headlines and large color photos; it has several daily supplements on sports, entertainment, and so forth, and most importantly, it has no discernable political orientation, which is perhaps the secret of its success. It is characterized as pluralistic and has columnists from both the right and left of Israel's political spectrum.

Herut [Freedom]

Herut, which first appeared in 1948 and folded in 1965, was a right-wing nationalist newspaper and was considered the inheritor of *Hamashkif*, despite the fact that it began publication several months before the latter ceased publication. When the State of Israel was founded, the underground movements disbanded their operations. The decision to establish *Herut* was the result of a debate between former leaders of the underground and leaders of the Revisionist movement.

Its first issue, in October 1948, consisted of twenty pages of articles written by the leaders of the movement. Despite its loyalty to the underground, the newspaper made serious efforts to avoid internal struggles. One of its daily columns published articles from other newspapers that attacked the Revisionist Movement and the underground.

The editors of *Herut* had hoped to publish a nonpolitical newspaper that would favor the political right while at the same time gathering readers from other political segments of the society. However, the political events during the State's early years consolidated *Herut* as an extreme opposition newspaper. It expressed criticism against the Labor-led government on all fronts and warned about future eventualities. The right-wing party, *Herut*, bearing the same name as the newspaper, funded it and oversaw its contents. Speeches by its leaders regularly appeared on its pages.

Its first-day issue sold about 20,000 copies but circulation swiftly dropped and stabilized at around 5,000. It has been argued that the relatively low circulation was due to the fact that some potential readers feared losing their jobs because of the dominance of the Labor government in those days.

In contrast with its initial goals, *Herut* remained a small newspaper that lacked much influence. Its main objective was to survive financially. Shutting down the newspaper was considered following each parliamentary election because of its heavy burden on the party till. Finally, at the end of 1965, following seventeen years of operation, the newspaper folded.

THE CONTENT ANALYSIS

In addition to selecting the four outstanding Nazi war crimes trials, it was necessary to determine the specific time periods for the content analysis. It was decided that the journalistic reporting to be studied should not be limited to the periods between the opening day of each of the trials and the days on which the respective verdicts were handed down. This was because the press had expressed interest in the trials even before they began and did not abandon them the moment the verdicts were handed down. Accordingly, the time frame was expanded to begin one month prior to the beginning of each trial and end one month following the verdicts. This made it possible to examine pre-trial as well as post-trial events and discussions, including the preparations for and the aftermath of the trials.

Based on these considerations, the following time frames were used for the four trials:

The Nuremberg trial: October 20, 1945 to November 1, 1946
The Eichmann trial: March 11, 1961 to January 15, 1962
The Auschwitz trial: November 20, 1963 to September 20, 1965
The Demjanjuk trial: January 16, 1987 to May 25, 1988

The comprehensive content analysis was carried out within these designated time frames. The initial plan of research called for the creation of a time-based sample of the newspapers in an attempt to represent as best as possible the complete array of items for the four trials. Fortunately, however, the funding for the study made it possible to work with the entire set of newspaper items, thereby avoiding the need to sample the material. Accordingly, all items dealing with the four trials were studied using a broad inclusion rule. This included news reports, background stories, essays, editorials, commentaries, letters to the editors, as well as photographs and cartoons.

In order to systematically cover the reporting of the four Nazi trials, a two-level codebook was developed. In the first level, each item was categorized and coded as a complete unit. This analysis consisted of various formal features of the items, such as size and placement, as well as broad categories of themes, emotional content, and their general tone. The second level was created in order to analyze the reporting in greater depth and detail. In this level the coding was based on individual statements. Each statement was determined by its author and subject matter. When one of these two components changed, a new statement was thus identified.

An analysis at the statement level was done in order to determine the exact thematic aspects and values in the reporting on the trials. The category system was established on the basis of theoretical and empirical assumptions after carefully studying excerpts from the actual reports of the trials, and partly on the basis of what was conceived as plausible. In addition to categories that were proposed with certainty, others were included whose occurrences were assumed and perhaps expected, but not assured. This was done under the assumption that it would indeed be meaningful even when certain statements were expected in a particular context but did not occur. See the complete codebook in the Appendix.

PROBLEMS IN PORTRAYING THE HOLOCAUST

Conducting a content analysis of the press on the subject of the Holocaust is likely to raise certain problems that might not exist in other content areas. Attempting to comprehend and analyze what really happened during the Holocaust could create much difficulty. In fact, most historians and others who have written about the Holocaust did not experience it first hand. A recurring theme in many survivors' stories is that even while the atrocities were taking place, they could not believe it was really happening (Browning, 1992). Therefore the media might be severely limited in their attempts to accurately present the reality of the Holocaust. These obstacles may be summarized in five major areas: terminology, oversimplification, trivialization, instrumentalization, and mystification.

Terminology

Writing about the events of the Holocaust presents a tough challenge. Its reality is above all imagination, and as Dekoven-Ezrachi (1980) pointed out, even realism caves in amidst reality. Human imagination, after Auschwitz, is not the same as before. The addition of *Auschwitz* to the dictionary means that today things are known that could not be fathomed in the past. Writing about the Holocaust dwarfs linguistic resources and threatens to defeat them. Wiesel (1978) claims that transforming the experience of the Holocaust into words has only one result, namely, distortion. Friedlander (1984) adds that the Holocaust provides only shadows or myths, because its reality was so extreme that language could not represent it faithfully. Guri (1963), in describing his book *In Front of the Glass Cell*, which deals with the Eichmann trial, wrote: "This book is nothing but a desperate attempt to grasp the immeasurable" (p. 284).

Journalists covering the Holocaust also felt the futility of language. Noah Kliger of *Yedioth Aharonoth* devoted an article to this subject on March 4, 1987 titled: "As if We Are Talking About Damaged Merchandise." Kliger complained about the use of words, terms, and definitions as if they were referring to the delivery of damaged merchandise that should have been destroyed, saying: "It is clear that even those whose eyes saw the atrocities, cannot turn them into words or explanations. . . . The brain and imagination simply refuse to accept the report of atrocities and language is anyhow too poor to describe them."

The Holocaust also has its own vocabulary. Words such as *Kapo* or *Sonderkommando* have no translation, as they are unprecedented in human experience. They indicate not only the functioning and daily routine of prisoners, but also a new hierarchy of human relations, values, and expectations (Dekoven-Ezrachi, 1980). Moreover, the exclusivity of the language does not come to the fore only in specific words such as the above. According to Segev (1994b), journalistic writing about the Holocaust is replete with eloquent speech. It is a different language, and at least in Hebrew, it conveys a biblical or a poetic lamentation. It is a different planet with respect to language, too.

Oversimplification

Simplistic generalizations concerning the Holocaust were prevalent especially during the first years after it ended. One of the most common statements was about the passiveness of the Jews during the war. Although this myth has been shattered, it is still widely accepted by the majority (Bauer & Lowe, 1981). Another example is the provision that all of Europe was against the Jews. This kind of statement detaches the subject from the facts and ignores all those who did not cooperate with the Nazis (a large part of Bulgarian and Romanian Jewry were saved as were most French Jews). Bauer (1990), who raised this topic, points out that the reason for this is the enormous fury that the Holocaust provokes. Because most Nazis are no longer alive, the anger is directed towards the world.

Trivialization

Part of the misgiving in the attempt to describe the Holocaust is trivialization (Ozick, 1969). Doneson (1985) explains that trivialization occurs when continuous repetitions turn something special into something trite. When popular culture is used in order to disseminate information about the Holocaust, its popularization or even worse—its trivialization—is inevitable.

One of the attempts to use popular culture was the book *Maus* by Spiegelman, the first edition of which appeared in 1986. The book presents events of the Holocaust in comic-strip form in which the Jews are depicted as mice, the Germans as cats, and the bystanders as pigs. It is the story of the author's attempt to extract information from his father about what happened to him during the Holocaust. Many attacked the book claiming that it is disrespectful, trivial, and desecrates the memory of the dead. Others, including White (1992), believe that it does not miss the point but rather presents the subject in an unusual and fascinating manner. White admits that this was one of the most touching testimonies he had ever read on the subject. In his view, *Maus* is a masterpiece of style and allegory that succeeds despite the use of a low style for the description of monumental events.

Instrumentalization

Instrumentalization of the Holocaust occurs when it is used for political purposes such as relating present events to Nazi deeds of the past. This issue emerged in Israel for the first time when Menachem Begin took office as Prime Minister in 1977. According to Keren (1985), ever since that time, mentioning the Holocaust has become commonplace and has served to stress extreme social and political views. During the Demjanjuk trial, according to Caspi (1988), there were only few among the journalists and the public who could free themselves from transient considerations and draw a distinction between the trial and its historical significance, on the one hand, and its actual political lessons, on the other hand.

Vidal Naquet (1989) goes even further in arguing that the Holocaust ceased to be historical reality and became a banal means of political legitimization. This topic arose in Israel in order to force political consensus or apply pressure on Jews in the Diaspora so that they would agree with political measures taken by Israel. There is evidence for this phenomenon on both sides of the Israeli political spectrum. The right compares the PLO to the Nazis and the left refers to certain actions that some Israelis do in the occupied territories as Nazi-like. Vidal Naquet adds that manipulation of Holocaust events for pragmatic purposes undermines their historical significance, transforms them into something unrealistic, and by so doing cooperates with the revisionists.

Mystification

This problem was considered closely by Bauer (1982). In his view, the first source for mystification was an improper use of the term

"Holocaust." Can it be used for other ethnic groups as well as Jews (for example, the murder of Poles and Lithuanians, discrimination against blacks in the United States and the Arabs in the West Bank) or should it be reserved as a unique concept? Survivors in particular were opposed to such comparisons, which were made in the name of freedom, equality, and justice. For them the Holocaust is something sacred, beyond imagination, incomprehensible. This notion poses a certain difficulty because if there is no way to know about the issue, most people will dismiss it as irrelevant.

Another problem in this context, raised by Eckardt and Eckardt (1978), is the danger of referring to the Holocaust as a unique episode of insanity and presenting it as a deviation or cultural mutation. This, in their view, will undermine its universal and historical importance. Only by trying to understand the events by means of comparisons or universalization can one make the Holocaust meaningful in an historical and human context (Doneson, 1985). Bauer (1982) concludes by saying: "one who does not acknowledge the fact that the situation of the Jews was unique—distorts history. On the other hand, those who say that the Holocaust has no parallel whatsoever and is impossible to explain—are also at fault in mystifying the issue" (pp. 75-76).

Friedlander (1977) follows this line of thought, although the dilemma he presents is a bit different; namely, should one avoid generalization and banality or should the Holocaust become such a special event in human history that it cannot be given any meaning at all? Friedlander's solution is not to avoid explanation, as partial as it may be, of cumulative historical trends. The importance of understanding the events was also brought up by Funkenstein (1989), who argued that all efforts should be taken to analyze the issue and search for answers, especially if similar acts are to be prevented in the future.

Another form of mystification brought up by Bauer (1982) is the inclination felt among current historians to deny some of the basic facts. This applies not only to Neo-Nazis but also to allegedly respectful and serious sources. A third form of mystification involves two contradictory aspects. On the one hand, there is the tendency to make Holocaust events into something allegorical, a symbol that can lead to transforming the whole issue into a myth or empty universal generalizations. On the other hand, there is a kind of "scientific" or "academic" approach that distances itself from the depths of the Holocaust, thereby creating "Holocaustology"—like a subdivision of history, on the same level as research concerning the silk industry in France during Mercantilism. In other words, people are "taught to erase the Holocaust without shedding even one tear" (p. 81).

Finally, Eisner (1983) presents a series of myths related to the Holocaust: that only a few hundred, or at most a few thousand Germans were responsible for the mass destruction; that the Jews went passively like sheep to slaughter; that survival tactics prevalent before the war such as assimilation, minimal visibility, and negotiating with gentiles could have saved the Jews; and the most vicious myth of all, that simply states that the Holocaust never really happened. Doneson (1985) points out a contrasting phenomenon of demystification where nothing is sacred: the boundaries between private and public are broken down because of the obsessive need of the individual to expose himself.

CODING PROCEDURE AND STATISTICAL ANALYSIS

Given the voluminous number of items to be coded, it was decided to hire several coders in each country. This was done in order to avoid as much as possible fatigue and instrument decay. Hebrew-speaking students did the coding of the Israeli items in Israel and German students in Germany did the coding of the German items. The coders were given several training sessions at which they learned the codebook, as well as the coding and notation procedures. Practice sessions were held until the coders reached a high level of proficiency. Given the nominal categories of most of the variables, estimates of reliability were calculated on the basis of percentage of agreements among the coders. The level of reliability obtained was a function of the nature of variables being measured. For some, no subjective judgment was allowed and the reliability was exceedingly high; for others, where subjective latitude in measurement was permitted, the reliability was lower. This should be taken into consideration, of course, when evaluating the findings.

Finally, the fact that the entire population of newspaper items was analyzed, rather than only a sample, negated the need to use statistical tests of significance when comparing the data across the two dimensions of the study: the four trials and the two countries. The findings of the study are presented in the following chapter.

5

Press Coverage of the Trials

The findings of the study are presented in the following tables and figures. As noted, the entire population of newspaper items was coded and analyzed, hence no sampling was done and accordingly no statistical tests of significance were required nor calculated. Most of the findings are presented in percentages, thus enabling comparisons between the four trials in the two countries. The percentages are presented with a precision of one digit beyond the decimal point; therefore the total percentages are sometimes slightly higher or lower than 100.

The findings are divided into several sections: (a) extent of the coverage; (b) characteristics of the items; (c) salience of the items; (d) the phases of the trials; (e) themes of the coverage by items; (f) themes of coverage by statements; (g) metaphors and loaded terms; (h) emotional tone of the items.

THE EXTENT OF THE COVERAGE

The first step in presenting the data of the content analysis was to describe the scope and extent of the coverage of the four Nazi trials in both countries. The amount of space given to the trials in the various newspapers can be viewed as a measure of the "agenda setting" of the trials; that is, as an estimate of the importance attributed by the editorial staffs to the trials.

Overall Coverage of the Trials

Three sets of data were used: the overall number of items; the mean number of items during the course of each of the trials; and the total space of all the items. Table 1 presents the overall number of items pertaining to the trials in the various newspapers.

In all the German newspapers studied there were 3,567 items about the trials compared with 5,673 items in all the Israeli newspapers. These figures alone should not give the impression, however, that there was greater coverage in Israel, because on average more newspapers per trial were examined in Israel. Nevertheless, the greater number of items in Israel is maintained even when the mean number of items per newspaper is calculated: 892 items per German newspaper and 1,135 items per Israeli newspaper. It should also be noted that there was considerable variability among the newspapers within each of the two countries.

An examination of the data reveals significant differences among the four trials in the two countries. In the German press the largest number of items was published about the Nuremberg trial and the Auschwitz trial received the second largest number of items. Perhaps the great attention given to these trials was due to the fact that they were conducted in Germany. The Eichmann trial was only in third place, with the least coverage going to the Demjanjuk trial. Clearly and quite understandably the German press and (probably) its public were most interested in the trials that took place in Germany.

A similar but reversed phenomenon occurred in Israel, with the trials conducted there arousing the greatest interest in the press (and probably among the public). Nearly 55% of all the items were concerned with the Eichmann trial, with the Demjanjuk trial in second place. The Nuremberg trial came third, with the Auschwitz trial in last place.

In Germany the *Nürnberger Nachrichten* and the *Tagesspiegel* published the largest number of items about the Nuremberg trial, 42% and 28% respectively. Perhaps the great attention in Nuremberg had to do with the fact that the trial against the chief war criminals was being conducted there, but it was not merely a local event, which can clearly be seen by the fact that it was also covered across Germany. It became no doubt a national news event. By contrast the number of items about the Nuremberg trial was smaller in the *Frankfurter Rundschau* and the *Süddeutsche Zeitung*, even though both appeared in the American zone and were thus subject to the same informational politics. Among the German newspapers *Die Welt* published the largest number of items about the Eichmann trial, followed by the *Frankfurter Allgemeine*. The *Frankfurter Allgemeine* and the *Frankfurter Rundschau* published the largest numbers of items about the Auschwitz trial—once again, news-

Table 1. Number of Newspaper Items Concerning the Trials.

	Nürnberger Nachrichten	Tages-spiegel	Die Welt	Frankfurter Allgemeine Zeitung	Süddeutsche Zeitung	Frankfurter Rundschau	Total	Average
				GERMAN NEWSPAPERS				
Nuremberg Trial	722	481	-	-	216	317	1,736	434
Eichmann Trial	-	-	242	227	178	140	787	197
Auschwitz Trial	-	-	202	317	181	233	933	233
Demjanjuk Trial	-	-	25	5	53	28	111	28
Total	722	481	469	549	628	718	3,567	-

	Hatzofeh	Hamashkif	Herut	Yedioth Aharonoth	Ha'aretz	Davar	Total	Average
				ISRAELI NEWSPAPERS				
Nuremberg Trial	179	141	-	44	252	181	797	159
Eichmann Trial	589	-	737	577	767	447	3,117	623
Auschwitz Trial	171	-	115	76	109	87	558	112
Demjanjuk Trial	107	-	-	482	310	302	1,201	300
Total	1,046	141	852	1,179	1,438	1,017	5,673	-

papers from the city in which the trial took place. Although the *Frankfurter Allgemeine*, the *Frankfurter Rundschau*, and (by far) *Die Welt* published considerably more items about the Auschwitz trial than the Eichmann trial, the *Süddeutsche Zeitung* published an equal number in both trials. The *Süddeutsche Zeitung* carried the largest number of items about the Demjanjuk trial—almost half of all the items about that trial in the four German newspapers—while the *Frankfurter Allgemeine* hardly covered it at all. Omitting the Nuremberg trial, and taking the other three trials together, which were all covered by "national" newspapers, the largest number of items appeared in the *Frankfurter Allgemeine Zeitung* (549), followed by *Die Welt* (469), the *Süddeutsche Zeitung* (412), and the *Frankfurter Rundschau* (401). It seems that these differences should be attributed more to differences in the types of newspapers than to their political orientations.

In Israel, *Ha'aretz* published the largest number of items about the four trials, followed by *Yedioth Aharonoth* and *Hatzofeh*. *Ha'aretz* led in the Nuremberg and Eichmann trials, *Hatzofeh* in the Auschwitz trial, and *Yedioth Aharonoth* in the Demjanjuk trial. It is interesting that *Yedioth Aharonoth* reported the least about the earliest and the most about the last of the four trials; perhaps its position as a popular daily reflected the change in the Israeli public's relation to the Holocaust more clearly than the other newspapers. Although the Israeli newspapers reported on the Eichmann trial with more or less the same (if not equal) frequency, there were greater differences pertaining to the other trials. Thus, for example, *Yedioth Aharonoth* published relatively few items about the Nuremberg and Auschwitz trials, and *Hatzofeh* published relatively few items about the Demjanjuk trial.

Continuity of Coverage

The four trials were lengthy ones: the Nuremberg trial lasted 12 months, the Eichmann trial took 10 months, the Auschwitz trial dragged on for 22 months and the Demjanjuk trial proceeded for 16 months. Every judicial process usually consists of several phases that occur in a fixed sequence. It is thus unreasonable to expect that the press would cover each phase with equal interest and intensity. Instead, it could be expected that the coverage of the trials by the press would be sporadic and uneven, depending to a large extent on the stages of the trials and of particular developments that might have occurred in each of them.

In order to assess the pattern of the coverage of the four trials over time, four figures are presented, one per trial, each depicting the mean number of items per month in Germany and Israel. The four figures suggest some similarities, although clearly there was nothing identical in the patterns of coverage. In all cases there seems to be a great increase in the coverage during the first few days and weeks of the trials, followed by an overall decline, with minor peaks appearing from time to time. Towards the end of the trials as the verdicts approached and were handed down there was once again more interest by the press, which was indicated by greater coverage.

The coverage of the Nuremberg trial ran in quite a uniform course in both countries, even when taking into account the different number of items (Figure 1). The first high point in Germany came in November and in Israel in December 1945, and in both countries a high point occurred in October 1946 at the end of the trial. Between these dates the coverage was generally steady, consisting of an average of about 30 to 40 articles per month in Germany and about 10 to 20 in Israel. In more than a few newspaper editions (mainly in the *Nürnberger Nachrichten* and the *Tagesspiegel*) the reader could find several items referring to the trial.

The Eichmann trial also evidenced a certain similarity in its course in the two countries (Figure 2). But the uneven intensity of the coverage in Israel led to a steeper ascent and a correspondingly steeper decline (after June 1961). In Germany the high point occurred in April (the opening month of the trial) and in Israel in May 1961. By May the German newspapers had published between a mean of 40 to 60 items per month. In Israel there were at times more than twice as many. After the court adjourned on August 14th of that year little was reported about the Eichmann trial between September and November, until December when the sentencing created another peak.

The coverage of the Auschwitz trial, on the other hand, was much more uneven (Figure 3). After an initial high point, reached in

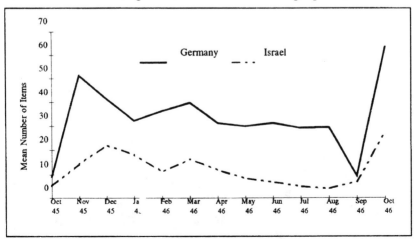

Figure 1. Mean number of items per month during the Nuremberg trial by country

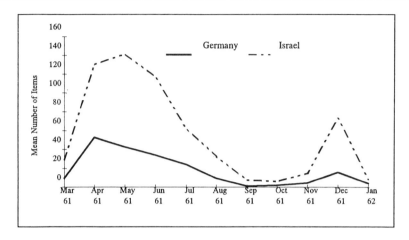

Figure 2. Mean number of items per month during the Eichmann trial by country

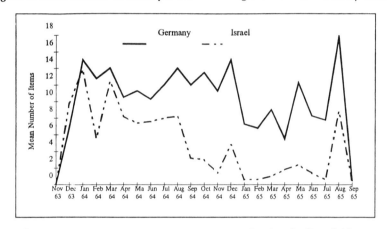

Figure 3. Mean number of items per month during the Auschwitz trial by country

January 1964, the number of items fluctuated from month to month. Even so, the coverage had consistent continuity. This is true, at least, with regard to the German newspapers, in which the coverage over the course of the entire year never went below a mean of ten items a month. On the other hand, the interest of the Israeli press in the long-running Auschwitz trial was discontinuous. Comparatively much was reported about the initial phase of the trial (until August 1964), but then interest waned sharply and didn't really rise again until the end (August 1965).

Israeli coverage over the course of the Demjanjuk trial proved to be on the whole far more substantial (Figure 4). However the variation in the number of items was greater than among the German papers and there were also some discontinuities. The highest point of the coverage

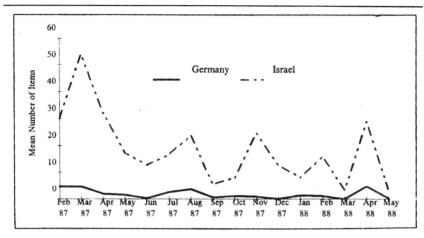

Figure 4. Mean number of items per month during the Demjanjuk trial by country

in Israel occurred in March 1987 shortly after the trial began, followed by smaller peaks in August and November 1987 and in April 1988; the low points occurred in June and September 1987 and in January and March 1988. The variations can essentially be attributed to events of the trial. Due to the overall small number of items in the German newspapers there seems to be no point in referring to "high points" altogether.

Space Allocated to the Trials

The extent of the coverage of the four trials can be inferred not only from the number of items, but also from the space allotted to them in the newspapers. The space of the items, calculated in square centimeters, is presented in Table 2.

Whereas the ratio between the German and Israeli newspapers in covering the trials based on the number of items is 44% to 56%, the ratio by amount of space devoted to the items is 40% to 60%. By this measure the preponderance of reporting in Israel is even somewhat higher, although the ranking among the trials did not change. The outstanding position of the Eichmann trial in Israel is even more evident not only in the total space devoted to it, but also in the average space per item—about 273 square centimeters—and the average item size in covering the Demjanjuk trial was not far behind with 240 square centimeters. In the German newspapers, once again the Nuremberg trial received the most space, followed by the Auschwitz trial, which was, however, on average somewhat more extensively reported. It should be noted that over the years the number of pages in the newspapers of both countries increased, as did the size of headlines and the use of photos, a fact which might explain some of the shift to larger items.

Table 2. Scope of Coverage (in Square Centimeters).

GERMAN NEWSPAPERS

	Nürnberger Nachrichten	Tages-spiegel	Die Welt	Frankfurter Allgemeine Zeitung	Süddeutsche Zeitung	Frankfurter Rundschau	Total	Average
Nuremberg Trial	104604	92145	-	-	66331	97868	360948	208
Eichmann Trial	-	-	31223	42364	32852	21920	128359	163
Auschwitz Trials	-	-	37438	98791	29158	35561	200948	215
Demjanjuk Trial	-	-	1808	2997	4118	2934	11857	107
Total	104,604	92,145	70,469	144,152	132,459	158,283	702,112	-

ISRAELI NEWSPAPERS

	Hatzofeh	Hamashkif	Herut	Yedioth Aharonoth	Ha'aretz	Davar	Total	Average
Nuremberg Trial	26657	18709	-	7660	25107	21293	99426	125
Eichmann Trial	148475	-	145357	253835	153078	150253	850998	273
Auschwitz Trials	20278	-	10645	26962	13970	9952	81807	147
Demjanjuk Trial	19439	-	-	107890	80810	80504	288643	240
Total	214,849	18,709	156,002	396,347	272,965	262,002	1,320,874	-

Based on the measurements of space allocated to the items, the relative position of the different newspapers changed to some extent. Thus the dominance of the *Nürnberger Nachrichten* during the Nuremberg trial was reduced and the *Süddeutsche Zeitung*, which published only 12% of the German items, constituted 18% of the space. *Die Welt* contained the largest number of items about the Eichmann trial, but the *Frankfurter Allgemeine*, with fewer but longer items, devoted more space to the trial. This was equally true for the *Süddeutsche Zeitung*. The *Frankfurter Allgemeine* achieved even greater priority with regard to the Auschwitz trial; its items took up almost half the space devoted to reports of this trial in the German newspapers. The *Frankfurter Rundschau*, which devoted the second largest amount of space to the Nuremberg trial among the four German newspapers, devoted the least amount of space to the Eichmann trial and was third with regard to the other two trials. The Demjanjuk trial was dealt with in only 3.1% of the German items and took up only 1.6% of the space. Moreover, the dominant role of the *Süddeutsche Zeitung* decreased somewhat; it published a greater number of items, but they were short, whereas the items in the *Frankfurter Allgemeine* were fewer in number but longer.

In Israel, across all four trials *Yedioth Aharonoth* devoted more space to the trials than any other newspaper and was in first place in all trials except the Nuremberg trial, which was led by *Hatzofeh*. *Yedioth Aharonoth* devoted above-average space particularly to the Eichmann trial and following *Yedioth Aharonoth*, *Hatzofeh* gave the most space to the Auschwitz trial, whereas *Ha'aretz* devoted the most space to the Demjanjuk trial.

CHARACTERISTICS OF THE ITEMS

The items that appeared in the newspapers were of different types and came from a variety of sources.

Types of Items

As for the type, the items could be any of the following: news reports, feature stories, editorials, letters to editors, interviews, poll results, trial documentation, citations from other media, photographs, and cartoons. Table 3 presents the distribution of the various types of items for the trials in both countries.

It is obvious that the overwhelming preponderance of the items would be news reports: 81% of all the items in Israel and 71% in Germany. Feature stories were more prevalent in the German newspa-

Table 3. Type of Item (in Percent).

	Nuremberg Trial n = 1736	Eichmann Trial n = 787	GERMAN NEWSPAPERS Auschwitz Trial n = 933	Demjanjuk Trial n = 111	Total n = 3567
News Report	71	72	68	88	71
Feature/Background	8	7	23	8	12
Editorial	9	8	4	2	7
Letter to Editor	1	6	1	1	2
Interview	-	-	-	-	-
Poll Results	-	-	-	-	-
Documentation	6	5	2	1	5
Reference to Other Media	1	-	1	-	1
Photo	3	1	1	-	2
Other	-	1	1	-	1
Total	99	100	101	100	101

Table 3. Type of Item (in Percent). (con't)

	Nuremberg Trial n = 791	Eichmann Trial n =3110	ISRAELI NEWSPAPERS Auschwitz Trial n = 554	Demjanjuk Trial n = 1193	Total n =5650
News Report	86	80	73	64	81
Feature/Background	9	6	10	15	6
Editorial	-	2	3	6	2
Letter to Editor	-	3	1	1	2
Interview	-	1	-	4	1
Poll Results	-	1	-	1	1
Documentation	2	4	2	-	4
Reference to Other Media	1	2	7	5	2
Photo	1	1	2	-	2
Other	1	-	1	3	-
Total	100	100	99	99	101

pers, particularly regarding the Auschwitz trial. To some extent the newspapers also published original source material and trial-related documents which included, for example, excerpts of the charges and summations or written evidence which appeared in 5% of the German items and in 4% of the Israeli items. In Germany relatively more documentary evidence was published about the Nuremberg trial, and in Israel, more about the Eichmann trial. Of the documentary material published in the newspapers, trial transcripts were most prominent, virtually all in Israel (9% of all documentation in the Auschwitz trial, 4% in the Demjanjuk trial, and 2% each in the Nuremberg and Eichmann trials). Other documentary evidence was presented in miniscule amounts.

It is also noteworthy that the trials received relatively more editorials in the German press (7%) compared with only 2% in the Israeli press. And yet, in Germany the trend for editorials decreased over the years whereas in Israel it increased. Interviews and opinion surveys did not appear in the German press and only very infrequently in the Israeli newspapers.

Finally, in both countries only 2% of the items were letters to editors. In Germany most of the letters (n = 46) were written about the Eichmann trial, whereas the Israeli newspapers published over 100 letters about the Eichmann and Demjanjuk trials but almost none about the trials held in Germany. In any event, because it is not known how many letters were received by the newspapers but not published, such letters can only be indirectly interpreted as an indication of public discussion provoked by the trials. It does seem justified, however, to assume that the Eichmann trial was a high point in both countries.

Photos

Photos in newspapers can often be powerful illustrations of the topic being presented. Although as Table 4 has indicated, only 2% of the items in each of the countries were photos; that is, the entire item being a photo, many of the other items included photos; some even included more than one photo (see Table 10). Table 4 presents the subjects in all the photos that appeared in the items.

The most striking overall finding was that the photos in the German press focused on the perpetrators of the crimes, whereas in the Israeli press they focused primarily on the Holocaust victims. Moreover, there were even relatively more photos of the defendants in Israel than there were of the witnesses in Germany. This phenomenon was especially evident in the coverage of the Eichmann and Demjanjuk trials. During the Auschwitz trial, however, photos of the defendants were first ranked in the Israeli newspapers as well (and almost so in the Nuremberg trial).

Table 4. Subjects of Photos (in Percent).

		GERMAN NEWSPAPERS			
	Nuremberg Trial $n = 258$	Eichmann Trial $n = 67$	Auschwitz Trial $n = 89$	Demjanjuk Trial $n = 9$	Total $n = 423$
Defendant(s)	40	39	33	56	38
Prosecution	5	9	1	-	5
Defense	14	2	-	-	10
Witness(es)	7	11	15	11	9
Judge(s)	7	2	5	11	5
Courtroom and People	13	14	12	11	13
Courtroom/Courthouse	2	8	5	11	4
Other Persons	5	11	12	-	7
Photos of Holocaust	7	3	18	-	9
Other	-	-	-	-	-
Total	100	99	101	100	100

Table 4. Subjects of Photos (in Percent). (con't)

	Nuremberg Trial n = 29	Eichmann Trial n = 553	Auschwitz Trial n = 74	Demjanjuk Trial n = 397	Total n = 1053
			ISRAELI NEWSPAPERS		
Defendant(s)	38	13	41	22	19
Prosecution	3	6	-	3	4
Defense	7	3	-	9	5
Witness(es)	-	24	5	25	22
Judge(s)	-	4	1	4	4
Courtroom and People	3	15	4	13	14
Courtroom/Courthouse	-	1	3	1	1
Other Persons	-	4	7	3	3
Photos of Holocaust	41	7	15	3	7
Other	7	23	24	18	21
Total	99	100	100	101	100

In addition, during the Nuremberg trial the Israeli press highlighted photographs of Holocaust scenes, more than in any of the later trials, even though the absolute number was rather small.

The number of photos of prosecuting and defense attorneys differed from trial to trial. In Germany, the defense attorneys for the Nuremberg trial were pictured noticeably more often than were the prosecutors; this was reversed for the Eichmann trial. The prosecutors of the Eichmann trial were more frequently pictured in Israel; the relationship was reversed for the Demjanjuk trial. There were no photos of the adversarial attorneys in the Demjanjuk trial in Germany and in the Auschwitz trial in Israel. Finally, photos of scenes of the Holocaust (e.g., death camps) served to illustrate the coverage. Whereas the relative proportion of Holocaust scenes was slightly greater in Germany, the absolute numbers were much higher in Israel (108 photos) compared with only 36 photos in the German newspapers.

SOURCES OF THE ITEMS

It was also of interest to determine the sources of the items; that is, who wrote the items, whether they were derived from news agencies or from the newspaper's own correspondents, and so forth. Table 5 presents information regarding the sources of the newspaper items.

The source of the material was quite different for each of the four trials as well as between the two countries. Whereas most items in Germany came either from news agencies or the newspaper reporters themselves, in Israel the source of nearly one third of the items was unidentified. This was probably due to the fact that in the earlier days Israeli newspapers did not use bylines for many of their items. This was mainly the case with the Eichmann and Nuremberg trials. In Germany, most of the items, especially in the Nuremberg trial came from news agencies, because there were few German reporters who could attend the trials. This also suggests that the Allies consigned the coverage of the Nuremberg trial primarily to DANA, the only news agency in the American-occupied zone at the time which, as a central institution, was more easily controlled, thereby enabling extensive conformity in the depiction of the trials. In Israel the reliance on the agencies for both trials that took place in Germany was mainly due to financial reasons. It should be noted that the Israeli news agency ITIM was established in 1950 after the Nuremberg trial; thus the Israeli newspapers had to rely for that trial on foreign news agencies such as the British Reuters or the American Associated Press and United Press. Also, the newspapers in both countries rarely used guest columnists.

Table 5. Source of Items (in Percent).

GERMAN NEWSPAPERS

	Nuremberg Trial n = 1736	Eichmann Trial n = 787	Auschwitz Trial n = 933	Demjanjuk Trial n = 111	Total n = 3567
Newspaper Journalist	18	38	76	16	37
News Agency	75	51	18	73	55
Guest Columnist	1	9	2	1	3
Unidentified	6	2	3	9	4
Other	1	1	1	1	1
Total	101	101	100	100	100

ISRAELI NEWSPAPERS

	Nuremberg Trial n = 782	Eichmann Trial n = 3100	Auschwitz Trial n = 557	Demjanjuk Trial n = 1193	Total n = 5632
Newspaper Journalist	18	38	76	16	37
Newspaper Journalist	14	35	17	56	34
News Agency	51	18	69	27	29
Guest Columnist	6	5	2	5	5
Unidentified	27	43	11	11	31
Other	2	-	1	2	1
Total	100	101	100	101	100

Although about half of the items on the Eichmann trial in the German newspapers originated in a news agency, 38% were written by their own correspondents. In fact, the four newspapers sent reporters to Israel, which clearly indicated that covering the Eichmann trial from its location was judged to be a political as well as a journalistic imperative. However, due to the length of the trial, these correspondents could not stay in Israel for its entire duration.

The situation was different with regard to the Auschwitz trial, which took place in Germany, thus enabling the German press much independent coverage. The reverse was true, however, for the Demjanjuk trial: the German newspapers relied heavily on materials provided by news agencies, although by then they all had their own permanent correspondents in Israel. This, too, in addition to the lesser space devoted to it, is further indication of the limited interest this trial had in Germany.

SALIENCE OF THE ITEMS

Next to be considered is the salience of the items in their respective newspapers. Salience was examined by means of five variables: size of the item, placement of the item, size of the headline, number of columns, and use of photos. The assumption was that these factors are indicators of the perceived importance and newsworthiness of the items, both from the journalists' and readers' perspectives. After separately presenting each of the salience factors, a salience index composed of all five is presented.

Size of Items

In addition to the overall space devoted by all the newspapers (Table 2), it was decided to examine the distribution of the size of each specific item. The items were accordingly divided into seven categories ranging from very short to very long items. Table 6 presents the distributions that reconfirm the finding that in the Israeli press a larger number of items and more space were devoted to the Nazi trials. For example, 12% of the Israeli items are larger than 500 square centimeters compared with only 6% in the German newspapers.

The differences between the two countries were especially notable in some of the trials. Thus during the Eichmann trial 16% of the Israeli items were larger than 500 square centimeters compared with only 3% in the German press and for the Demjanjuk trial the difference

Table 6. Size of Newspaper Items by Trials (in Percent).

GERMAN NEWSPAPERS

Square Centimeters	Nuremberg Trial $n = 1736$	Eichmann Trial $n = 787$	Auschwitz Trial $n = 933$	Demjanjuk Trial $n = 111$	Total $n = 3567$
up to 20	10	8	1	13	7
21 to 50	15	20	9	39	15
51 to 100	16	16	15	23	16
101 to 200	23	27	35	14	27
201 to 500	29	27	33	9	29
501 to 1000	6	2	6	2	5
1001 and more	2	1	1	1	1
Total	101	101	100	101	100

ISRAELI NEWSPAPERS

Square Centimeters	Nuremberg Trial $n = 734$	Eichmann Trial $n = 3096$	Auschwitz Trial $n = 555$	Demjanjuk Trial $n = 1185$	Total $n = 5570$
up to 20	13	5	6	1	5
21 to 50	29	20	25	12	20
51 to 100	22	18	31	22	21
101 to 200	17	21	23	27	22
201 to 500	15	21	9	28	20
501 to 1000	3	10	5	8	8
1001 and more	1	6	2	2	4
Total	100	101	101	100	100

was 10% versus 3% respectively. On the other hand, 13% of the German items during the Demjanjuk trial were very small (up to 20 square centimeters) compared with only 1% in the Israeli newspapers.

Placement of the Items

The placement of the items in the newspapers was classified into one of five categories: the main headline story, a front-page item, an item in a special section devoted to the trial, an item appearing in a supplement, and an item on any other page of the newspaper. The data appear in Table 7.

Overall, the placement of the items relating to the war crimes trials was in more salient places in the Israeli press compared with the German press. Thus 42% of all the Israeli items appeared either on the front page of the newspapers or in a special section devoted to the trials, compared with only 31% in the German newspapers.

As for the specific trials, the placement in Germany of items of the Nuremberg trial is particularly striking: 7% were main headline stories, just under one-third appeared on the front page, and 22% even appeared on a special page. This placement is of course attributable to the Allied Press Authority, whose aim was to make the German public aware of the trials, thus making it difficult for readers to avoid coverage of the trials, even if they had a psychological disposition to do so. During the Eichmann trial, German newspapers were no longer subject to external supervision and displayed a different pattern: only 1% (8 items) were main headline stories, but 102 items (13%) appeared on the front page, with the majority of the items appearing on other pages. The placement of reports about the Auschwitz trial was even more reserved: it received no main headline and only 6% of the items appeared on the front page. Of the 111 items on the Demjanjuk trial, 14% appeared on the front page and the rest on other pages.

The Nuremberg trial received prominent placement in the Israeli press as well: although only 3% of the items made the main headline, two-thirds appeared on the front page (it should be noted that at the time some of the pre-State Israeli newspapers consisted of only 2-4 pages, hence the increased likelihood of appearing on the first page). This was true for "only" 29% of the items on the Eichmann trial, although the absolute number of items was much greater. In addition, special pages and supplements were sometimes dedicated to it (6% during the Eichmann trial). Assuming that the "other page" placement indicates less importance, the Auschwitz trial was the least prominently displayed in the Israeli press. Even so, nearly one-third of the relevant items appeared on the front page, compared with only 6% in Germany.

Table 7. Placement of Item (in Percent).

	GERMAN NEWSPAPERS				
	Nuremberg Trial $n=1736$	Eichmann Trial $n=787$	Auschwitz Trial $n=933$	Demjanjuk Trial $n=111$	Total $n=3567$
Main Headline	7	1	-	-	4
Front Page	31	13	6	14	20
Special Page	22	1	1	-	11
Supplement	6	2	-	-	3
Other Page	35	84	92	87	62
Total	101	101	99	101	100

	ISRAELI NEWSPAPERS				
	Nuremberg Trial $n=790$	Eichmann Trial $n=3104$	Auschwitz Trial $n=555$	Demjanjuk Trial $n=1194$	Total $n=5643$
Main Headline	3	4	-	1	3
Front Page	63	29	31	5	29
Special Page	-	6	1	44	13
Supplement	-	2	2	6	3
Other Page	34	59	65	43	53
Total	100	100	99	99	101

The Demjanjuk trial, which received great attention in Israel, published 44% of the items about this trial on special pages, and an additional 6% in supplements, but only 5% on the front page, in marked contrast with the other trials. This is at least in part a function of the format of the newspaper that tended to devote special sections to important topics.

Size of Headlines

Salience is also a function of the size of the headline. Headlines are very important as they often serve as a trigger to get the attention of the reader. The height of the letters used in the headlines was measured in millimeters (see Table 8).

There is a striking difference in the size of the headlines between the German and Israeli newspapers. In general, there were no overall differences in the percentage of small headlines in the two countries. However, the Israeli newspapers had relatively many more large headlines, whereas the German newspapers had relatively more medium-size headlines. Although the distributions of headline size in both countries during the Nuremberg trial were quite similar, during the Demjanjuk trial, 42 years later, the headlines in Israel were strikingly larger. This may be due to two factors: the relatively great continuing interest in Nazi war crimes trials in the Israeli press, as well as the fact that some of the Israeli newspapers, including *Yedioth Aharonoth* (which had the greatest number of items during the Demjanjuk trial) tended to become more tabloid in format, hence the larger headlines.

Column Width of Items

The column width of the items is another component of salience. Here reference is made to items that are limited to one column, wherever they are placed, versus items that span several columns, up to the width of the entire page of the newspaper. Table 9 presents the distribution of the items by their column width.

The data indicate that whereas in Germany no item was wider than five columns, in Israel 9% of all the items (over 500 items) appeared across six or more columns, including 2% (about 110 items) being spread across the whole width of the page (8 or 9 columns, depending on the newspaper). Whereas there is some degree of similarity between the two countries regarding the Nuremberg trial, the Demjanjuk trial reveals a significant difference. In the latter case, 75% of the German items were placed in a single column, whereas in Israel most were multicolumn items. This could possibly be explained, as noted earlier, at least in part,

Table 8. Height of Headline Letters, in Millimeters (in Percent).

	GERMAN NEWSPAPERS				
	Nuremberg Trial $n=1736$	Eichmann Trial $n=787$	Auschwitz Trial $n=933$	Demjanjuk Trial $n=111$	Total $n=3567$
up to 4 mm	44	42	32	65	41
5 to 10 mm	52	58	68	35	57
11 mm and more	4	-	-	-	2
Total	100	100	100	100	100
	ISRAELI NEWSPAPERS				
	Nuremberg Trial $n=797$	Eichmann Trial $n=3117$	Auschwitz Trial $n=558$	Demjanjuk Trial $n=1201$	Total $n=5673$
up to 4 mm	48	48	62	14	42
5 to 10 mm	44	30	25	49	36
11 mm and more	8	22	13	37	22
Total	100	100	100	100	100

Table 9. Column Width of Items (in Percent).

	GERMAN NEWSPAPERS				
	Nuremberg Trial $n = 1736$	Eichmann Trial $n = 787$	Auschwitz Trial $n = 933$	Demjanjuk Trial $n = 111$	Total $n = 3567$
One column	44	38	17	75	36
Two columns	34	35	48	14	38
Three columns	16	24	32	7	22
Four columns	5	2	2	3	3
Five columns	1	1	1	1	1
Six columns	-	-	-	-	-
Seven columns	-	-	-	-	-
Eight columns	-	-	-	-	-
Nine columns	-	-	-	-	-
Total	100	100	100	100	100

Table 9. Column Width of Items (in Percent). (con't)

	Nuremberg Trial $n = 797$	Eichmann Trial $n = 3118$	Auschwitz Trial $n = 558$	Demjanjuk Trial $n = 1199$	Total $n = 5672$
		ISRAELI NEWSPAPERS			
One column	31	31	31	17	28
Two columns	39	33	46	23	33
Three columns	16	13	14	24	16
Four columns	8	7	3	23	10
Five columns	2	5	3	6	5
Six columns	2	3	1	4	3
Seven columns	1	6	1	2	4
Eight columns	1	1	-	1	1
Nine columns	2	-	-	1	1
Total	102	99	99	101	101

by the tabloid nature of some of the Israeli press during the period of the Demjanjuk trial, which has a tendency to print larger and bolder items spanning across the page, as well as the greater interest in the trial in Israel.

Number of Photos and Cartoons

The final component of salience used in the study was the use of photos and cartoons. The assumption is that the presence of such illustrative material contributes to the overall attention paid to the items. Table 10 presents the data on the photos and cartoons.

Ten percent of the German items contained photos or cartoons compared with 15% in the Israeli press. In Germany, the Nuremberg trial, the first war crimes trial held, was most heavily illustrated, whereas in Israel, the Demjanjuk trial, the last one conducted, was the most heavily illustrated. This very large increase in the use of visual illustrations in the Israeli coverage of the Demjanjuk trial is probably due to the significant growth of photojournalism in Israel, which is exhibited by more photos in general in Israeli newspapers. And yet, when taking into account the absolute number of photos, the Eichmann trial was the most heavily illustrated in all the newspapers in both countries with more than 550 photographs.

The Salience Index

In determining the overall salience of the items, an index was calculated based on the five components with equal weights assigned to each. The scope of the item was divided into four levels and each of the other variables was divided into three levels. Thus the lowest index score per item could be 5 and the highest could be 16. The salience index is presented in two forms: as mean scores and in categories. Table 11 presents the mean salience scores for the four trials in both countries.

The mean salience scores quite expectedly reinforce the findings concerning the five individual components of salience. The overall mean salience score of the Israeli newspapers was higher than that of the German newspapers, thus indicating that the Israeli newspapers did more to direct the attention of their readers to the Nazi trials than did the German newspapers for German readers. The salience score was higher in Israel for the Nuremberg trial (albeit only slightly), as well as for the Eichmann trial and especially for the Demjanjuk trial. Only the Auschwitz trial received a higher salience score in Germany.

Table 10. Number of Photos and Cartoons (in Percent).

	GERMAN NEWSPAPERS				
	Nuremberg Trial $n=1736$	Eichmann Trial $n=787$	Auschwitz Trial $n=933$	Demjanjuk Trial $n=111$	Total $n=3567$
None	88	92	93	93	90
One	10	7	6	6	8
Two or More	2	1	2	1	2
Total	100	100	101	100	100

	ISRAELI NEWSPAPERS				
	Nuremberg Trial $n=737$	Eichmann Trial $n=3117$	Auschwitz Trial $n=558$	Demjanjuk Trial $n=1199$	Total $n=5671$
None	97	87	93	73	86
One	3	10	5	24	12
Two or More	-	3	2	4	
Total	100	100	100	101	101

Table 11. Mean Salience Scores.

| | GERMAN NEWSPAPERS | | ISRAELI NEWSPAPERS | |
	no. of cases	mean score	no. of cases	mean score
Nuremberg Trial	1,736	8.75	722	8.88
Eichmann Trial	787	7.94	3,070	9.14
Auschwitz Trials	933	8.49	549	8.25
Demjanjuk Trial	111	6.79	1,166	9.98
Total	3,567	8.44	5,507	9.20

The salience index was also divided into four categories: Low (scores of 5-7), medium-low (8-9), medium-high (10-11), and high (12-16). Table 12 presents the breakdown for the four levels.

Correlated with the previous table, more items in the German newspapers were in the low and medium-low categories (74%) compared with the Israeli newspapers (55%). Conversely, Israeli newspapers had more items in the two higher salience categories (45%) compared with Germany (26%). In Germany the items with higher salience scores were mostly associated with the Nuremberg trial and in Israel with the Demjanjuk trial, which even exceeded the salience scores of the Eichmann trial.

THE PHASES OF THE TRIALS

Every trial, including those of Nazi war crimes, goes through various phases that would naturally be reflected in their coverage by the press. Table 13 presents the distributions of the items according to the different phases.

The focal point of the coverage, without exception, was the testimony of the witnesses. This trend was far stronger in Germany with nearly half the items, compared with Israel, where only one-third of the items reported on witnesses' testimony. In the German newspapers almost two-thirds of the coverage of the Auschwitz and Demjanjuk trials concentrated on the witnesses, which also constituted the longest phase of the trial, and nearly one-half of the items on the Nuremberg trial dealt with this phase. On the other hand, less than one-third of the items of the Eichmann trial dealt with the witnesses.

This suggests a different thematic emphasis of the Eichmann trial compared with the three other trials. This is supported by the fact

Table 12. Salience Scores by Category (in Percent).

GERMAN NEWSPAPERS

	Nuremberg Trial n = 1722	Eichmann Trial n = 784	Auschwitz Trial n = 931	Demjanjuk Trial n = 111	Total n = 3548
Low	33	38	16	70	31
Medium-low	29	47	70	19	43
Medium-high	31	12	12	9	21
High	7	3	2	2	5
Total	100	100	100	100	100

ISRAELI NEWSPAPERS

	Nuremberg Trial n = 722	Eichmann Trial n = 3070	Auschwitz Trial n = 549	Demjanjuk Trial n = 1166	Total n = 5507
Low	25	29	39	13	26
Medium-low	39	26	32	30	29
Medium-high	27	25	22	33	27
High	9	20	8	25	18
Total	100	100	101	101	100

Table 13. The Main Stages of the Trials as Depicted in the Newspaper Items (in Percent).

	GERMAN NEWSPAPERS				
	Nuremberg Trial $n = 1736$	Eichmann Trial $n = 787$	Auschwitz Trial $n = 933$	Demjanjuk Trial $n = 111$	Total $n = 3567$
Pre-trial preparations	8	13	1	3	7
Reading of indictment	1	2	1	3	1
Opening statement of the prosecution	4	3	-	-	3
Examination of the defendant(s)	5	12	8	-	7
Opening statement of the defense	-	-	-	-	-
Testimony of witnesses	46	30	65	62	48
Summation by the defense	4	1	6	1	4
Summation by the prosecution	3	2	4	3	3
Closing words of the defendant(s)	1	-	1	1	1
Verdict	-	3	-	8	1
Sentencing	3	2	3	6	3
Irrelevant to the trial	9	25	6	9	12
Post-trial discussions	11	4	2	1	7
Not identified	4	4	2	4	4
Total	99	101	99	101	101

Table 13. The Main Stages of the Trials as Depicted in the Newspaper Items (in Percent). (con't)

	Nuremberg Trial n = 778	ISRAELI NEWSPAPERS Eichmann Trial n = 3103	ISRAELI NEWSPAPERS Auschwitz Trial n = 552	ISRAELI NEWSPAPERS Demjanjuk Trial n = 1189	Total n = 5622
Pre-trial preparations	5	6	4	1	5
Reading of indictment	5	3	1	1	2
Opening statement of the prosecution	7	1	-	-	2
Examination of the defendant(s)	6	10	15	1	8
Opening statement of the defense	1	-	-	1	1
Testimony of witnesses	26	27	43	51	34
Summation by the defense	-	1	1	4	1
Summation by the prosecution	5	2	2	3	3
Closing words of the defendant(s)	3	1	2	1	1
Verdict	3	4	2	4	4
Sentencing	1	2	1	3	2
Irrelevant to the trial	9	27	6	16	20
Post-trial discussions	13	3	4	3	4
Not identified	17	13	19	11	13
Total	101	100	100	100	100

that one-fourth of the items on the Eichmann trial had no direct relevance to it. Thus the Eichmann proceedings provided an occasion for newspaper items that only indirectly depicted the trial but were in one way or another determined by it. Also, the German newspapers devoted relatively more items to the buildup surrounding the Eichmann trial than to the other trials as well as in comparison with the Israeli press.

In Israel, too, there was a relatively great emphasis in the newspapers placed on the evidence given by the witnesses, which was particularly manifest in the Demjanjuk and Auschwitz trials. The coverage of the Eichmann and Nuremberg trials also placed significant emphasis on the witnesses, but the relative position of this element was lower given the other focal points. Thus in Israel, too, the Eichmann trial seems to have been given a different thematic perspective, not just as a judicial event, but as an opportunity to raise other questions. To some extent, this was also the case in the Israeli coverage of the Demjanjuk trial. The proportion of items dealing with nonwitness matters was noticeably small.

Several additional observations are noteworthy. In both countries the Nuremberg trial received the largest number of items after the trial was over, suggesting that not everything had already been said by the time the verdict was delivered. Also, summations for the defense for the first three trials were hardly reported, especially in Israel, whereas the summations for the prosecution were more prevalent. Finally, in Israel there were more items about the verdicts (as a separate phase of the trial), whereas it was barely mentioned as a separate phase in Germany, except in the case of the Demjanjuk trial.

THE THEMES OF THE COVERAGE: ANALYSIS BY ITEMS

After discussing the formal and structural characteristics of the coverage of the trials, attention now shifts to their specific contents. More than 30 different themes were identified and included in the content analysis. These can be summarized in six main thematic groups: (a) themes relating to the charges brought against the defendants (e.g., war crimes, annihilation and genocide); (b) themes relating to the trial procedure (e.g., preparation for the trials and the behavior of the defendants); (3) themes relating to the historical causes of the Holocaust (e.g., the situation leading up to World War II and anti-Semitism); (4) themes relating to the political situation at the time of the trials (e.g., the relations between Germany and Israel and public opinion in the two countries); (5) moral issues relating to the Holocaust (e.g., education and/or the responsibility of the Germans); and (6) themes relating to the Holocaust survivors (e.g., their emotional or physical condition).

If an item contained more than one theme, all were coded. The complete array of 9,240 items in the study yielded a total of 27,582 references to themes. As there were more items in the Israeli newspapers studied, almost twice as many themes emerged there (9,266 in Germany and 18,316 in Israel).

Examining the distributions of the six thematic groups indicates that two themes dominated the newspaper coverage of the trials: the charges and procedural matters (see Table 14). The dominance of these themes is not surprising, of course, given that the subject was criminal trials. In Germany 58% of the items were concerned with the charges against the defendants compared with 46% in Israel. Also, 25% and 29% of the items in the two countries, respectively, dealt with the progress of the proceedings. This picture holds true, even if not equally pronounced, for the first three trials. In the Demjanjuk trial, however, there were more items about the procedures than about the charges in both countries.

The other four theme categories were of less prominence in the coverage of the trials. Historical issues, such as the causes of the Holocaust, were dealt with in 7% of the German and in 5% of the Israeli items. The political situation during the trials was an issue in 11% of the Israeli items and in 6% of the German items. Moral issues and the condition of the survivors received only minimal mention, albeit no less than that of historical topics, with the latter theme being almost entirely absent in the German coverage.

As for the specific trials, during the Eichmann trial the German press coverage paid relatively more attention to historical themes, the political situation, and moral issues. The political situation was relatively high on the agenda in the Israeli coverage of the Eichmann trial, as was the case in the German press. The condition of the survivors received above-average coverage in the Israeli newspapers mainly during the Auschwitz trial, and historical themes were prominent in the Israeli press only during the Nuremberg trial.

An additional analysis was conducted on the themes, in an attempt to identify the main foci of the items. Accordingly, for each item the coders were instructed to identify the single most dominant theme. The coders also had the option of determining that the item had no main theme. Table 15 presents the distributions of the major thematic categories.

The first point that emerges in the data is the fact that in 28% of the German items and in 17% of the Israeli items there was no discernable main theme. The data also show that overall the legal issues constituted the focal point of the Israeli coverage in all but the Auschwitz trial, far more than in Germany. In Germany, the main theme also pertained to legal issues in the two trials held in Israel, but in the two German tri-

Table 14. Major Thematic Categories (in Percent).

GERMAN NEWSPAPERS

	Nuremberg Trial n = 4145	Eichmann Trial n = 2213	Auschwitz Trial n = 2698	Demjanjuk Trial n = 210	Total n = 9266
The charges	66	42	62	42	58
Legal issues	22	28	25	47	25
Historical issues	6	10	6	1	7
Political situation during trials	4	14	3	7	6
Moral issues	2	5	1	1	3
Condition of Holocaust survivors	0	2	3	2	1
Total	100	101	100	100	100

ISRAELI NEWSPAPERS

	Nuremberg Trial n = 2678	Eichmann Trial n = 10237	Auschwitz Trial n = 2250	Demjanjuk Trial n = 2851	Total n = 18316
The charges	45	48	52	36	46
Legal issues	30	25	25	44	29
Historical issues	13	4	4	2	5
Political situation during trials	6	14	7	6	11
Moral issues	5	4	3	4	4
Condition of Holocaust survivors	1	5	10	7	5
Total	100	100	101	99	100

Table 15. Major Thematic Categories by Items (in Percent).

GERMAN NEWSPAPERS

	Nuremberg Trial n = 1722	Eichmann Trial n = 784	Auschwitz Trial n = 931	Demjanjuk Trial n = 111	Total n = 3548
No major theme	25	31	27	62	28
The charges	39	22	46	11	36
Legal issues	27	29	17	25	25
Historical issues	4	4	4	1	4
Political situation during trials	4	10	3	1	5
Moral issues	2	3	1	-	2
Condition of Holocaust survivors	-	2	1	-	1
Total	101	101	99	100	101

ISRAELI NEWSPAPERS

	Nuremberg Trial n = 784	Eichmann Trial n = 3097	Auschwitz Trial n = 555	Demjanjuk Trial n = 1191	Total n = 5627
No major theme	12	19	13	15	17
The charges	25	12	38	5	14
Legal issues	45	37	35	65	44
Historical issues	10	6	1	1	5
Political situation during trials	5	18	9	6	13
Moral issues	4	6	2	5	5
Condition of Holocaust survivors	1	3	2	4	3
Total	102	101	100	101	101

als the main theme was the charges against the defendants. The other four themes appeared more sporadically. What is striking is the relatively large proportion of Israeli items whose focal point was the political situation, especially during the Eichmann trial. Moral aspects and the condition of the survivors were also more often the focal points in Israel than in Germany.

The thematic profile of the newspaper items concerning the Nazi war crimes trials becomes fully apparent when examining the relative frequency of all the 30 individual subthemes which are presented in Table 16A (for Germany) and 16B (for Israel). It should be noted that given the fact that more than one theme could appear in any item, no "total" is provided, as the totals by far exceed 100%.

Given the overwhelming differences among the four trials, it does not seem meaningful to compare overall percentages between the two countries. Nevertheless it can be seen that among the subthemes the extermination of Jews appeared most frequently in the German newspapers (in 31% of all items). This theme was even more pronounced in the Israeli press (in 41% of all items) but was not the most prevalent theme there; the course and development of the trial proceedings appeared in Israel most often (in 52% of all items). The third most frequently appearing Israeli theme concerned atrocities committed against Jews (28%), a theme depicted far less often in Germany (12%). However, the German press mentioned extermination of non-Jews to a far greater extent (24%) than did the Israeli press (6%).

In covering the Nuremberg trial the German press concentrated primarily on one point in the indictment; namely, the preparation for war (39%). This coincides with the fact that the Allies regarded this as the defendants' most serious crime. However, this hardly appeared in the three later trials. And although the murder of Jews appeared in 20% of the German items, the extermination of other people was given more prominence (23%).

In Israel, coverage of the Nuremberg trial took a clearly different stance. The preparation for and waging of war, which the Allies wanted to emphasize, was not the dominant theme. Instead, handling the proceedings, which appeared in 54% of the items, led the way followed by the extermination of Jews (30%), which was more pronounced than in the German press (20%). Clearly the Israeli agenda was more concerned with the fate of Jews than that of other victims of the war.

During the Eichmann trial extermination of the Jews became a main theme. The newspapers in both countries discussed this as one of the themes relating to the charges more than in any of the other trials. Covering the Auschwitz trial was quite different, however. In the Israeli newspapers the most prevalent topic was the extermination of people of

Table 16A. Themes Appearing in German Newspaper Items (in Percent).

	Nuremberg Trial n = 1722	Eichmann Trial n = 784	Auschwitz Trial n = 931	Demjanjuk Trial n = 111	Total n = 3548
The charges					
Preparation for war and warfare	39	2	-	1	19
Economic plundering	14	9	3	-	10
Discrimination against Jews	12	11	2	-	9
Deportation, forced labor of Jews	8	25	11	2	12
Extermination of Jews	20	53	33	48	31
Discrimination against others	12	-	1	-	6
Deportation, forced labor of others	16	3	18	-	13
Extermination of others	23	5	43	-	24
Description of atrocities	4	2	37	8	12
Crimes against humanity	1	1	-	2	1
Deportation, forced labor of unknown	2	1	6	-	3
Extermination of unknown	6	3	26	19	11
Other	1	2	-	-	1
Legal issues					
Preparation for the proceedings	5	7	1	12	5
Handling and course of the proceedings	21	37	38	47	30
Behavior of the defendant(s)	14	19	26	23	19
Residence of witnesses	2	11	4	2	5

Table 16A. Themes Appearing in German Newspaper Items (in Percent). (con't)

Evaluation of the verdict	5	3	3	4	4
Other	6	1	-	1	3
Historical issues					
Political, economic, and social situation	8	6	4	-	6
Anti-Semitism	2	8	1	1	3
Attitude of Germans	4	12	13	2	8
Other	-	1	-	-	-
Political situation during trials					
Relations between Germany and Israel	-	8	-	-	2
Public opinion in Israel	-	9	-	12	3
Public opinion in Germany	5	7	5	-	6
Public opinion in other countries	4	11	4	1	6
New outbreaks of anti-Semitism	-	3	-	-	1
Other	-	1	-	-	-
Moral issues					
Lessons to be drawn from the Holocaust	2	3	-	2	2
Responsibility of the Germans	3	11	3	-	5
Other	-	-	-	-	-
Condition of Holocaust survivors					
Life stories	-	4	4	2	2
Condition of Holocaust survivors	-	1	4	3	2
Other	-	-	-	-	-

Table 16B. Themes Appearing in Israeli Newspaper Items (in Percent).

	Nuremberg Trial $n = 797$	Eichmann Trial $n = 3118$	Auschwitz Trial $n = 554$	Demjanjuk Trial $n = 1185$	Total $n = 5654$
The charges					
Preparation for war and warfare	19	1	1	1	4
Economic plundering	9	13	7	4	10
Discrimination against Jews	18	16	8	10	14
Deportation, forced labor of Jews	11	27	17	11	20
Extermination of Jews	30	51	38	24	41
Discrimination against others	4	2	2	2	2
Deportation or forced labor of others	4	3	4	2	3
Extermination of others	9	4	17	2	6
Description of atrocities	14	30	60	17	28
Crimes against humanity	6	4	1	3	4
Deportation, forced labor of unknown	5	1	17	1	3
Extermination of unknown	12	6	65	6	13
Other	11	1	3	2	3
Legal issues					
Preparation for the proceedings	6	7	9	4	4
Handling and course of the proceedings	54	45	63	67	52
Behavior of the defendant(s)	24	13	27	15	17
Residence of witnesses	2	7	2	3	5

Table 16B. Themes Appearing in Israeli Newspaper Items (in Percent). (con't)

Evaluation of the verdict	8	8	7	13	8
Other	8	5	2	2	3
Historical issues					
Political, economic, and social situation	14	4	2	1	4
Anti-Semitism	10	3	3	1	3
Attitude of Germans	11	4	3	1	4
Other	9	4	7	2	6
Political situation during trials					
Relations between Germany and Israel	-	3	6	1	4
Public opinion in Israel	1	3	11	10	9
Public opinion in Germany	6	15	7	1	6
Public opinion in other countries	8	7	14	1	10
New outbreaks of anti-Semitism	2	2	4	1	3
Other	3	2	4	2	3
Moral issues					
Lessons to be drawn from the Holocaust	4	3	4	5	4
Responsibility of the Germans	9	10	6	2	6
Other	4	3	4	2	3
Condition of Holocaust survivors					
Life stories	2	19	10	9	10
Condition of Holocaust survivors	2	10	5	8	6
Other	-	-	-	-	-

unknown identity, followed by, but in similar frequency, the handling of the proceedings and the descriptions of atrocities. In the German press, too, the extermination of other people (not necessarily Jews) was the most frequent topic during the Auschwitz trial, although to a lesser extent than in Israel. During the Demjanjuk trial the German newspapers discussed most frequently the extermination of Jews and the trial proceedings. Trial proceedings were also the main focus of the Israeli press.

The atrocities committed by the defendants and their accomplices were emphasized in different ways in the two countries. In Germany, atrocities were mentioned in 12% of the items compared with 28% in the Israeli items. It seems that the question of the waging of the war was more important than the factory-like execution of innocent people. Only during the Auschwitz trial were the horrifying aspects of the Holocaust forcefully presented to the German public in 37% of the items, whereas in the other trials minimal coverage was devoted to the topic.

This was different in Israel, where the depiction of atrocities was given more prominence. During the Auschwitz trial, in 60% of the items reference was made to atrocities, and in the Eichmann trial 30% of the items contained such references. In the Nuremberg and Demjanjuk trials there was also more mention of atrocities than in the German press. Not only were atrocities more frequently mentioned in the Israeli press but they were also described in more detail, especially regarding the Auschwitz trial, about which even the German newspapers published relatively more details.

The handling of the proceedings was the most important legal issue in Israel, even more than in Germany. Over half of the Israeli items on the Nuremberg trial, just under half on the Eichmann trial, and about two-thirds on the Auschwitz and Demjanjuk trials dealt with the course of the proceedings. Questions about the handling of the proceedings were more salient in the Israeli press than in Germany. The discrepancy in this regard between the newspapers of the two countries was greatest during the Nuremberg trial and least during the Eichmann trial. The German coverage detailed the course and conduct of the Demjanjuk trial relatively more frequently than the other trials. The treatment by the German newspapers of the defendants' behavior was comparatively greater during the Auschwitz and Demjanjuk trials than during the Eichmann trial and among the Israeli newspapers was greater during the Nuremberg and Auschwitz trials. This theme was of relatively equal prominence to both countries during the Auschwitz trial. A clear difference also emerges with regard to the evaluation of the verdict with the Israeli newspapers evidently more interested: between 7% and 13% of the items in Israel were concerned with the verdict, about twice as many as in Germany.

Apart from the Nuremberg trial, the Israeli press was less interested than its German counterpart in historical themes. The behavior of Germans during the Nazi regime, anti-Semitism in Germany, and the social, political, and economic situation before the Second World War were examined in Israel with relative frequency only in connection with the Nuremberg trial. In Germany it was the Eichmann trial in particular that raised questions regarding the causes of the Holocaust. The attitude of the Germans was the most frequent among the historical themes in both the Eichmann and Auschwitz trials. Except for the Eichmann trial, anti-Semitism was hardly ever offered as a cause of the Holocaust. In any event, the historical themes played only a minor role in the coverage of the trials in both countries.

References to the political situation at the time of the trials were more often made in Israel than in Germany. Except for the period during the Eichmann trial, relations between the two countries did not constitute a theme in the German press. The same was true for new indications of anti-Semitism at the time of the trial. In both countries there were reports of public opinion, especially in the countries in which the trials were taking place. There were also reports in the press of both countries about public opinion in other countries, excluding Germany and Israel, especially during the Eichmann trial. Generally speaking, however, interest in public opinion was greater in the Israeli press than in the German press.

Moral issues were not brought up often, but in general appeared more in the Israeli press than in the German press. Lessons to be drawn from the Holocaust hardly appeared in the German newspapers whereas in the Israeli newspapers there was a low but consistent reference during all the trials. As for the responsibility of the Germans for what had happened during the war, throughout the Eichmann trial 11% of the German items made such references but hardly at all during the other trials. In Israel, on the other hand, this was especially the case during the two trials held in Germany and less so during the trials held in Israel.

Finally, differences were also found in the coverage of the last thematic group, the life history and current life situation of the Holocaust survivors. In the course of the trials the German public got very little information about these people, whereas the Israeli press informed its readers about this to quite a large extent, most markedly during the Auschwitz trial.

Description of Atrocities

Atrocities committed by the defendants and their accomplices were mentioned more frequently in the coverage of the Israeli newspapers compared with the German press (see Table 17). The greatest emphasis on atrocities in the German press occurred during the Auschwitz trial, where 49% of the items had such references. In the other three trials mention of atrocities was much lower, ranging from 11% to 15%.

In Israel, the depiction of the atrocities was given a broader scope. During the Auschwitz trial 64% of the items made references to atrocities and 36% of the items did so during the Eichmann trial. The mentioning of atrocities in Israel during the Nuremberg and Demjanjuk trials also exceeded the mention of atrocities in the German press. Not only were atrocities more frequently mentioned in the Israeli press but they were also described in greater detail in all the trials. This was especially the case regarding the Auschwitz trial, which the German newspapers also emphasized.

References to Witnesses

Despite the emphasis on the testimony of witnesses, which appeared in about one-third of the items in both countries, Table 18 details some differences between Germany and Israel. In the German press more attention was paid to the biographical information concerning the witnesses, whereas the Israeli newspapers went more deeply into the evidence. In Germany only about 2% of the items dealt with the condition of the witnesses, whereas in Israel about 8% of the items made reference to it.

Reference to Number of Holocaust Victims

Using numbers is a typical journalistic device to suggest objectivity. Thus, mentioning the number of victims of the Holocaust could be an indication of the perceived severity of the phenomenon. More than 1,000 items in each of the two countries made reference to the number of victims, as can be seen in Table 19.

In slightly less than half the cases the Israeli newspapers spoke of millions of victims with the figure of "six million" being a common mantra. In the German newspapers such large numbers of victims were mentioned in only about one-third of the items with smaller numbers being cited more frequently. One possible interpretation is that this does not necessarily mean that the number of victims was downplayed but rather that the German newspapers dealt more often with individual victims or groups of victims, hence the total quantitative magnitude of the Holocaust was not discussed as often as in Israel. This kind of individualization can be found above all in the coverage of the Auschwitz trial (in both countries). By contrast, the greater number of victims—and

Table 17. Descriptions of Atrocities (in Percent).

GERMAN NEWSPAPERS

	Nuremberg Trial n = 1722	Eichmann Trial n = 784	Auschwitz Trial n = 931	Demjanjuk Trial n = 111	Total n = 3548
No atrocities mentioned	85	86	51	88	76
Atrocities mentioned with no details	11	11	31	6	16
Details of atrocities	4	3	18	5	7
Total	100	100	100	99	99

ISRAELI NEWSPAPERS

	Nuremberg Trial n = 799	Eichmann Trial n = 3066	Auschwitz Trial n = 551	Demjanjuk Trial n = 1177	Total n = 5573
No atrocities mentioned	76	65	37	80	67
Atrocities mentioned with no details	20	22	31	13	21
Details of atrocities	4	14	33	7	13
Total	100	101	101	100	101

Table 18. References to a Witness (in Percent).

GERMAN NEWSPAPERS

	Nuremberg Trial n = 1722	Eichmann Trial n = 784	Auschwitz Trial n = 931	Demjanjuk Trial n = 111	Total n = 3548
No witnesses mentioned	73	76	46	65	66
Only biographical facts mentioned	3	4	2	3	3
Biographical facts and testimony	19	16	44	27	25
Evidence	5	1	3	1	3
Mental and physical conditions	-	-	-	1	-
Evidence and mental/physical condition	1	-	2	-	1
Biography, condition, and evidence	-	2	3	4	1
Total	101	99	100	101	99

ISRAELI NEWSPAPERS

	Nuremberg Trial n = 774	Eichmann Trial n = 3074	Auschwitz Trial n = 548	Demjanjuk Trial n = 1179	Total n = 5585
No witnesses mentioned	74	70	46	49	64
Only biographical facts mentioned	3	4	2	4	4
Biographical facts and testimony	10	6	28	20	12
Evidence	11	14	15	11	13
Mental and physical conditions	-	1	1	2	1
Evidence and mental/physical condition	1	3	2	4	3
Biography, condition, and evidence	1	2	6	10	4
Total	100	100	100	100	101

Table 19. Reference to the Number of Holocaust Victims (in Percent).

GERMAN NEWSPAPERS

	Nuremberg Trial n = 340	Eichmann Trial n = 224	Auschwitz Trial n = 412	Demjanjuk Trial n = 55	Total n = 1031
Less than one thousand	20	8	43	-	25
One thousand to one hundred thousand	21	17	33	7	24
One hundred thousand to one million	10	13	9	89	14
One to six million	50	62	15	4	36
Total	101	100	100	100	99

ISRAELI NEWSPAPERS

	Nuremberg Trial n = 130	Eichmann Trial n = 621	Auschwitz Trial n = 236	Demjanjuk Trial n = 135	Total n = 1122
Less than one thousand	16	9	36	14	16
One thousand to one hundred thousand	28	20	26	10	21
One hundred thousand to one million	9	14	10	30	15
One to six million	48	57	27	47	48
Total	101	100	99	101	100

therefore, the total dimension of the Holocaust—was particularly in the foreground of the Eichmann trial.

THE THEMES OF THE COVERAGE: ANALYSIS BY STATEMENTS

The overall findings of the content analysis thus far suggest that the trial events were depicted in Germany more with a view to the defendants and in Israel to the victims. Thus, the German newspapers emphasized the crimes committed by Germans during the Nazi era, with the fate of the Jews being de-emphasized compared with the Israeli press. The questions relating to the causes of the catastrophe, the responsibility for it, and the lessons that could be drawn from it were only occasional topics of the German press. By contrast, the coverage in the Israeli newspapers concentrated much more on the Jewish victims and on the circumstances of the crimes.

As noted at the outset, the content analysis was done at two levels: by items and by statements. Having completed the presentation of the data by items, the following pages deal with the data on the basis of the analysis of the individual statements. Statements refer to assertions or remarks made by someone regarding one of the trials in connection with themes enumerated earlier. The analysis by statements makes it possible to go one step further in deepening the understanding of issues mentioned in the items. A statement is considered to be new when the person making it and/or its subject changes.

In all, 6,404 statements were identified in the items of the German newspapers and 9,759 for the Israeli newspapers. These 16,163 statements are the corpus for the detailed analysis. The proportion of the statements in both countries corresponds almost exactly to that of the items. Taking into account, once again, the number of newspapers in each country, the mean number of statements per newspaper in Israel was 1,952 compared to 1,601 in Germany. By far the largest number of statements in the German newspapers appeared during the Nuremberg trial (2,468), which was the most extensively covered trial in that country. This was followed by the Auschwitz trial (1,989 statements), the Eichmann trial (1,819 statements), and the Demjanjuk trial (128 statements). In Israel the greatest number of statements appeared in the items about the Eichmann trial ($n = 5,434$), which represent more than half of all the statements in the Israeli press on the four trials. Second in number of statements was the coverage of the Demjanjuk trial with 1,869 statements (a relatively small number compared with the extensive coverage of the trial), followed by the Auschwitz trial with 1,240 statements and finally the Nuremberg trial, which generated 1,220 statements.

Table 20 presents the distribution of the sources of the statements. The greatest number of statements in both countries (30% in Germany and 36% in Israel) came from the authors of items themselves; that is, reporters, editors, and so forth. The second most frequent source of statements in the German newspapers (22%) was the defendants. On average, every tenth statement came from a prosecutor (with decreasing frequency from trial to trial) or the defense, which on average was quoted as often. These were followed by witnesses (7%) and judges (5%). All other statements were attributed to a variety of sources, none greater, on average, than 3%. In Israel, too, the defendants stood in second place as the source of statements, but only in about half the frequency as in Germany. Also, the prosecutors were quoted twice as often in Germany and the proportion of statements by witnesses was largely the same.

There were some quite noticeable differences among the trials in both countries. Journalists in Germany were least frequent as authors of statements during the Auschwitz trial and most recurrent during the Demjanjuk trial. In the Israeli press, too, the authors were most salient in the coverage of the trials. In Germany, the defendants were heard more than the witnesses in all four trials, but in Israel during the Demjanjuk trial the witnesses were heard relatively more often. Moreover, in this case an above-average number of statements appeared by the defense. Statements by public figures were generally quite rare, but in the German press there were some statements attributed to German officials during the Eichmann trial and to Israeli officials during the Demjanjuk trial.

More than 100 statement categories were classified into eleven groups: metaphors of the Holocaust, motives for the trials, criticism of the trials, lessons to be learned from the Holocaust, legal aspects of the proceedings, characteristics of the defendants, guilt and responsibility, causes of the Holocaust, analogies of the Holocaust, anti-Semitism, and the evaluations of the verdicts. Table 21 presents the distributions of the statements in both countries.

The dominant subject of the statements in the German press was the characteristics and personality of the defendants, ranging from 65% of all the statements in the Auschwitz trial to 41% of all statements during the Eichmann trial. Other statements appeared much less frequently, with criticism of the trial in second place, followed by statements about motives for the trial and statements about aspects of responsibility. Only 5% or less of all statements concerned the other thematic areas. The largest number of statements about motives for the trials in the German newspapers concerned the Nuremberg and Eichmann trials, and the least amount of critical remarks concerned the Nuremberg trial. This may be due to the fact that at the time the Allies had control over the German press and did not want to allow criticism of the trials that they

Table 20. Sources of Statements (in Percent).

GERMAN NEWSPAPERS

	Nuremberg Trial n = 2468	Eichmann Trial n = 1819	Auschwitz Trial n = 1989	Demjanjuk Trial n = 128	Total n = 6404
Author of item	35	30	22	42	30
Judge	6	4	5	11	5
Prosecution	14	9	8	2	10
Defense	7	13	12	13	10
Defendant(s)	20	16	31	14	22
Witness	3	6	15	4	7
Israeli public official	-	2	-	6	1
German public official	3	7	-	-	3
Public official of other county	2	1	1	1	1
Expert	1	-	-	-	-
Israeli public	-	2	-	2	1
German public	4	1	2	-	3
Public of other countries	1	-	-	1	1
Israeli media	-	1	-	1	-
German media	-	1	-	-	-
Media of other countries	4	3	2	-	3
Other	2	4	2	3	3
Total	102	100	100	100	100

Table 20. Sources of Statements (in Percent). (con't)

	Nuremberg Trial n = 1220	ISRAELI NEWSPAPERS Eichmann Trial n = 5434	Auschwitz Trial n = 1240	Demjanjuk Trial n = 1869	Total n = 9759
Author of item	47	35	34	35	36
Judge	4	2	3	4	3
Prosecution	9	5	4	5	5
Defense	5	9	3	21	10
Defendant(s)	18	11	19	6	12
Witness	4	5	18	15	8
Israeli public official	-	3	-	4	2
German public official	2	3	2	-	2
Public official of other country	3	4	2	2	3
Expert	1	2	2	3	2
Israeli public	-	2	1	2	2
German public	1	3	7	-	2
Public of other countries	-	3	-	1	2
Israeli media	-	-	-	-	-
German media	1	1	-	-	1
Media of other countries	3	8	2	1	5
Other	3	5	4	4	4
Total	101	101	101	103	99

Table 21. Statement Categories (in Percent).

	GERMAN NEWSPAPERS				
	Nuremberg Trial $n = 2468$	Eichmann Trial $n = 1819$	Auschwitz Trial $n = 1989$	Demjanjuk Trial $n = 128$	Total $n = 6404$
Metaphors of the Holocaust	1	3	3	2	3
Motives for the trials	11	10	5	8	9
Criticism of the trials	9	20	18	22	15
Lessons from the Holocaust	1	1	-	-	1
Legal aspects	8	6	3	7	6
Characteristics of defendant(s)	48	41	65	56	52
Guilt and responsibility	9	12	2	-	7
Causes of the Holocaust	2	3	1	-	2
Analogies	1	-	-	-	1
Anti-Semitism	-	2	-	-	1
Evaluation of the verdict	9	1	2	5	5
Total	99	99	99	100	102

Table 21. Statement Categories (in Percent). (con't)

	ISRAELI NEWSPAPERS				
	Nuremberg Trial $n = 1220$	Eichmann Trial $n = 5434$	Auschwitz Trial $n = 1240$	Demjanjuk Trial $n = 1869$	Total $n = 9759$
Metaphors of the Holocaust	3	8	8	7	7
Motives for the trials	10	13	9	13	12
Criticism of the trials	13	14	18	37	18
Lessons from the Holocaust	3	3	5	5	4
Legal aspects	5	7	2	6	6
Characteristics of defendant(s)	34	27	40	22	28
Guilt and responsibility	16	15	14	3	13
Causes of the Holocaust	5	2	2	1	2
Analogies	-	1	-	-	1
Anti-Semitism	5	4	2	2	4
Evaluation of the verdict	3	3	3	3	3
Total	97	97	103	99	98

were conducting. The relatively largest number of statements concerning responsibility was also made with regard to the Eichmann trial. Evaluations of the verdict were noticeably frequent in the coverage of the Nuremberg trial but because of the small number of statements regarding the Demjanjuk trial it is difficult to compare it to the other three trials (only two themes—the personality of the defendant and criticism of the trial—made up most of its statements).

The Israeli newspapers, taken on the whole, did not have as dominant a subject of the statements as did the German newspapers. Indeed, the characteristics of the defendants was in the foreground there, too, but to a much lesser degree in comparison with Germany (with an average of 28%). On the other hand, there was greater variability of the statements across most of the possibilities, thus almost all the other groups of statements were more prevalent than in the German newspapers. In Israel, too, there were differences among the trials in the distribution of statements. The greatest number of statements concerning the characteristics of the defendants occurred during the Nuremberg trial (34%) and the fewest number of statements concerning the defendant appeared in the Demjanjuk trial (22%), the trial during which there was the most criticism expressed (37%). The German and Israeli newspapers differed considerably on this point with Israel taking the lead. Finally, whereas in Germany the verdicts of the four trials were assessed in statements that varied in frequency with each trial, in Israel the frequency of such statements was quite similar in all four cases.

Characteristics of the Defendants

Clearly, the dominant statement category in the entire coverage of the Nazi war crimes trials was the characteristics and personality of the various defendants. Table 22 presents the data.

This was the only instance in all the relevant categories in which more statements were made in Germany than in Israel. In Germany there were 3,305 statements compared with 2,762 statements in the Israeli press. This confirms once again the primacy of references to the defendants in the German newspaper coverage of the trials.

The emphasis in the German press and to a lesser extent in the Israeli press was on the defendants not being conscious of their guilt or actually denying it. During the Auschwitz trial, which produced the largest number of relevant statements, nearly half expressed this notion, as was the case during the Demjanjuk trial. The necessity to follow orders during a state of emergency was Eichmann's main defense strategy. The data support this notion (with 33% of the statements arguing that the defendant committed the crimes under orders to do so). And

Table 22. Statements Regarding Characteristics of the Defendants (in Percent).

	Nuremberg Trial n = 1187	GERMAN NEWSPAPERS Eichmann Trial n = 755	Auschwitz Trial n = 1291	Demjanjuk Trial n = 72	Total n = 3305
Conscious of guilt	17	5	11	1	12
Not conscious of guilt	35	21	49	49	38
Nonreactive to witnesses	5	5	1	13	4
Embarrassed after hearing witness	5	1	1	3	2
Indifference	4	-	-	-	2
Arrogance	2	-	1	-	1
Sadism	2	2	14	25	7
Criminal nature	1	-	2	-	1
Committed crime of free will	13	27	11	7	15
Committed crime to fulfill orders	15	33	10	-	17
Typical German	-	2	-	-	1
Not typical German	-	-	-	-	-
Other	2	3	1	1	2
Total	101	99	101	99	102

Table 22. Statements Regarding Characteristics of the Defendants (in Percent). (con't)

	Nuremberg Trial n = 412	ISRAELI NEWSPAPERS			Total n = 2762
		Eichmann Trial n = 1455	Auschwitz Trial n = 490	Demjanjuk Trial n = 405	
Conscious of guilt	9	4	8	3	5
Not conscious of guilt	23	12	16	25	16
Nonreactive to witnesses	3	4	4	3	4
Embarrassed after hearing witness	4	1	1	1	1
Indifference	3	5	3	7	5
Arrogance	3	2	2	-	2
Sadism	2	2	12	11	5
Criminal nature	10	5	10	19	9
Committed crime of free will	4	19	11	10	14
Committed crime to fulfill orders	7	27	14	3	18
Typical German	4	3	2	2	3
Not typical German	-	-	-	-	-
Other	28	17	17	17	18
Total	100	101	100	101	100

yet, this point was much debated by 27% of the statements suggesting that he actually committed the crimes of his free will. In addition, during the Auschwitz trial, and especially during the Demjanjuk trial, the sadistic tendencies of the defendants were mentioned. Indifference or dismay on the part of the defendant(s) was seldom or not at all noted; neither was arrogance. That the defendant exhibited typical German characteristics appeared as an assertion in the German press only a few times during the Eichmann trial.

The Israeli press stated much less often than the German press that the crimes were denied and no consciousness of guilt was shown. Such statements were most likely to be found during the Nuremberg and Demjanjuk trials. However, admission of guilt was also not often mentioned. In this regard statements about the necessity of following orders during a state of emergency appeared significantly often especially during the Eichmann trial (27%) and to a lesser extent during the Auschwitz trial (14%), and were almost nonexistent during the Demjanjuk trial (3%). In Israel, the criminal nature of the defendants was clearly pronounced, especially with regard to Ivan Demjanjuk. Comparable statements were hardly ever made in the German newspapers.

Motives for the Trials

Statements about motives for the trials were made about twice as often in the Israeli newspapers as in the German press (Table 23). Across all the trials in both countries the most frequently cited motive was the task of bringing criminals to justice. In second place in Germany was the motive of deterrence, whereas in Israel it was the motive not to forget the past. Other prominent German motives were educating the young generation, demonstrating the need for international law, and coming to terms with and atoning for the past. The moral obligation to the victims, deterrence, educating the young generation, and revenge were most often found in the Israeli newspapers. Also noteworthy is the difference between the relatively high level of atoning for the past in Germany and its low frequency in Israel.

Different motives were depicted for the various trials. In the coverage of the Nuremberg trial both countries focused on the trial for the sake of justice, the need for international law, and deterrence. In Israel, the need for justice was also the most frequently named motive during the Eichmann trial. In Germany, however, mention of this motive was exceeded by motives of educating the younger generation and atoning for the past. The motives next in rank in the German press during the Auschwitz trial were overcoming the past and atonement, and in Israel the struggle against forgetting the past. To avoid forgetting was

Table 23. Statements Regarding Motives for the Trials (in Percent).

	GERMAN NEWSPAPERS				
	Nuremberg Trial $n = 270$	Eichmann Trial $n = 182$	Auschwitz Trial $n = 104$	Demjanjuk Trial $n = 10$	Total $n = 566$
For the sake of justice	26	9	20	-	20
Moral obligations	6	4	4	10	4
Revenge, retribution	5	2	2	-	3
Deterrence	17	9	10	-	13
To come to terms with the past	4	13	13	10	8
To educate the young generation	6	17	8	40	10
To avoid forgetting the past	1	7	8	20	6
To atone for the past	8	6	13	-	8
To enhance Germany's current position	5	4	3	-	4
To enhance Israel's current position	-	8	-	10	3
To demonstrate Israel's strength	-	3	-	-	1
To influence world public opinion	-	8	1	-	3
To demonstrate international law	17	2	-	10	9
Other	4	9	15	-	8
Total	99	101	97	100	100

Table 23. Statements Regarding Motives for the Trials (in Percent). (con't)

	Nuremberg Trial n = 122	ISRAELI NEWSPAPERS			Total n = 1144
		Eichmann Trial n = 677	Auschwitz Trial n = 106	Demjanjuk Trial n = 241	
For the sake of justice	19	20	17	18	19
Moral obligation	6	9	10	10	9
Revenge, retribution	9	7	10	10	8
Deterrence	13	9	11	6	9
To come to terms with the past	1	2	2	2	2
To educate the young generation	7	12	8	15	9
To avoid forgetting the past	6	15	14	20	15
To atone for the past	2	3	2	1	2
To enhance Germany's current position	2	1	7	1	1
To enhance Israel's current position	1	3	1	1	2
To demonstrate Israel's strength	-	6	2	2	5
To influence world public opinion	6	8	3	4	6
To demonstrate international law	15	1	2	2	3
Other	15	6	11	6	8
Total	102	102	100	98	98

also the most frequently mentioned motive in Israel during the Demjanjuk trial followed by the sake of justice, educating the young generation, revenge, and moral obligation. In Germany, however, the number of statements during the Demjanjuk trial was too small for analysis.

Criticism of the Trials

Statements were also made criticizing the trials. These include concern about problems in the proceedings and the belief that the trials should not have been held altogether. In the Israeli press there were slightly more such statements ($n = 1,144$) than in the German press ($n = 968$) but in terms of the overall ratio of the number of items, the Israeli advantage was less than with most other variables.

As Table 24 indicates, in Germany the criticism was mostly directed toward the trial proceedings (29%). In Israel, too, this was the most common criticism, but only in 16% of the statements. The second most frequent criticism in Germany was the credibility of witnesses, which was also quite prevalent in Israel. In both countries few statements were made regarding such topics as the lack of public interest, danger of trivializing the Holocaust, the need to make a clean break with the past, the arousal of painful memories or antipathy, or the possibility that anti-Semitism would be revived.

Criticism of the Nuremberg trial was primarily legal in nature, focusing on the course of the proceedings, the jurisdiction of the court, the methods of investigation, and the legitimacy of retroactive legislation. This was true mainly for the German newspapers, although the Israeli newspapers shared this tendency as well. During the Eichmann trial there were not only many more critical statements but their contents were also more diverse. Whereas the most frequent criticism in Germany was still the course of the trial and the competence of the court, in Israel, the competence of the court and the capture of the defendant took precedence.

Whereas the revival of antipathy towards Germany was most feared by the German press during the Eichmann trial, compared with the other trials the course of the proceedings and the credibility of witnesses were stronger topics of criticism during the Auschwitz trial. In Israel, during the Auschwitz trial relatively much criticism was directed at the issue of statute of limitations as well as the lack of interest shown by the public in conducting the trial. In Israel, too, the course of the proceedings was the most frequent subject of criticism, but to a noticeably lesser extent than in Germany. Whereas the German criticism was predominantly directed toward legal issues, the Israeli criticism was more

Table 24. Statements Regarding Criticism of the Trials (in Percent).

	GERMAN NEWSPAPERS				
	Nuremberg Trial $n=212$	Eichmann Trial $n=372$	Auschwitz Trial $n=356$	Demjanjuk Trial $n=28$	Total $n=968$
No public interest	3	1	2	-	2
Trivialization of the Holocaust	-	3	2	4	2
Ending the debate about the past	-	2	4	-	2
Painful memories	-	5	-	-	2
Revival of animosity ag. Germany	-	11	2	-	5
Revival of anti-Semitism	-	2	-	-	1
Abducting the defendant(s)	-	10	-	-	4
Statute of Limitations	-	1	4	-	2
Legal standing	14	15	4	4	10
Legality of retroactive legislation	12	6	-	-	5
Voluminous material	2	1	3	-	2
Methods of investigation	1	-	2	4	1
Admissibility of documents	11	9	2	32	8
Credibility of witnesses	6	10	30	25	17
Course of the proceedings	35	20	35	21	29
Influence of the media	1	1	2	-	1
Other	12	-	9	11	7
Total	97	97	101	101	100

Table 24. Statements Regarding Criticism of the Trials (in Percent). (con't)

	Nuremberg Trial n = 161	ISRAELI NEWSPAPERS Eichmann Trial n = 751	Auschwitz Trial n = 170	Demjanjuk Trial n = 699	Total n = 1144
No public interest	6	1	10	2	3
Trivialization of the Holocaust	3	1	3	2	2
Ending the debate about the past	1	1	8	-	2
Painful memories	1	3	3	1	2
Revival of animosity ag. Germany	3	6	4	-	3
Revival of anti-Semitism	-	4	2	2	3
Abduction the defendant(s)	-	16	2	1	8
Statute of Limitations	1	2	13	1	3
Legal standing	10	20	4	4	11
Legality of retroactive legislation	6	6	4	1	4
Voluminous material	-	1	-	-	-
Methods of investigation	8	2	3	13	7
Admissibility of documents	3	8	4	25	14
Credibility of witnesses	2	4	9	18	10
Course of the proceedings	30	11	17	16	16
Influence of the media	2	-	2	3	3
Other	24	12	14	9	12
Total	100	98	102	98	103

strongly oriented toward the social milieu of the Federal Republic in which the trial was taking place.

Criticism relating to the proceedings played a substantial role in Israel during the Demjanjuk trial, in which doubts about the evidence, especially the validity of documents, the credibility of witnesses, the course of the trial, and the methods of investigation made up just under three-fourths of all critical statements. The competence of the court, which was a primary subject of criticism during the Nuremberg and Eichmann trials, was hardly mentioned during the other two trials.

Lessons from the Holocaust

As can be seen in Table 25, statements about possible lessons that could be drawn from the experience of the Holocaust were, as noted, very rare, but nevertheless seven times more frequent in the Israeli press ($n = 376$) than in the German press ($n = 52$).

In general, the German journalists clearly saw the trials as less of an occasion than did their Israeli counterparts to have the public learn lessons from the Holocaust. In fact, no references at all were made in the later two trials in the German press, and the references that did appear, albeit infrequently, were the importance of democracy (during the Nuremberg trial) and the need to resist fascism (during the Eichmann trial).

In Israel, most of the statements on lessons to be learned were made during the two trials conducted in Jerusalem. However, whereas during the Eichmann trial the greatest emphasis was on the dangers of a recurring Holocaust, during the Demjanjuk trial the most often mentioned lesson was the incomprehensibility of the Holocaust. Additional lessons that were repeatedly mentioned in Israel were the duty to resist fascism, the importance of Zionism, and the fact that spiritual strength and greatness instill courage.

Judicial Aspects of the Trials

Table 26 presents several categories of judicial aspects of the trials: Conducting them in the first place, the fairness of the proceedings, and the justification of capital punishment.

In both countries such statements were of secondary importance compared with other statement categories, and the overall ratio between Israeli and German statements was close to their respective total coverage of the trials. In Germany the conduct of the trial in accordance with regulations was more strongly emphasized than in Israel (especially

Table 25. Statements Regarding Lessons from the Holocaust (in Percent).

	Nuremberg Trial n = 29	Eichmann Trial n = 22	Auschwitz Trial n = 1	Demjanjuk Trial n = 0	Total n = 52
Tolerance towards minorities	-	-	-	-	-
The importance of democracy	41	14	-	-	29
The importance of Zionism	10	18	-	-	13
Obligation to resist fascism	21	41	-	-	29
Battling anti-Semitism	-	-	-	-	-
Avoiding judgment without experience	-	-	-	-	-
Strength and greatness instill courage	-	-	-	-	-
Holocaust beyond comprehension	-	-	-	-	-
Danger of recurrence of the Holocaust	10	9	-	-	10
No lessons possible	-	-	-	-	-
Other	17	18	-	-	19
Total	99	100	-	-	100

GERMAN NEWSPAPERS

Table 25. Statements Regarding Lessons from the Holocaust (in Percent). (con't)

	Nuremberg Trial n = 38	ISRAELI NEWSPAPERS			Total n = 376
		Eichmann Trial n = 182	Auschwitz Trial n = 61	Demjanjuk Trial n = 95	
Tolerance towards minorities	5	7	2	4	5
The importance of democracy	3	2	5	4	3
The importance of Zionism	16	16	-	16	13
Obligation to resist fascism	8	15	20	7	13
Battling anti-Semitism	11	5	7	15	9
Avoiding judgment without experience	-	6	2	5	5
Strength and greatness instill courage	-	9	10	5	10
Holocaust beyond comprehension	-	2	13	21	9
Danger of recurrence of the Holocaust	21	23	25	14	20
No lessons possible	3	1	-	2	1
Other	34	14	18	6	14
Total	101	100	102	99	102

Table 26. Statements Regarding Judicial Aspects of the Trials (in Percent).

GERMAN NEWSPAPERS

	Nuremberg Trial $n = 199$	Eichmann Trial $n = 108$	Auschwitz Trial $n = 52$	Demjanjuk Trial $n = 9$	Total $n = 368$
Sufficient legal basis for the trial	19	31	10	-	20
Fair and just procedures	67	39	83	56	61
Questioning capital punishment	11	29	8	44	17
Other	4	2	-	-	2
Total	101	101	101	100	100

ISRAELI NEWSPAPERS

	Nuremberg Trial $n = 66$	Eichmann Trial $n = 407$	Auschwitz Trial $n = 29$	Demjanjuk Trial $n = 118$	Total $n = 620$
Sufficient legal basis for the trial	19	13	14	15	14
Fair and just procedures	12	36	10	48	35
Questioning capital punishment	10	29	3	16	23
Other	59	22	72	20	28
Total	100	100	99	99	100

during the Nuremberg and Auschwitz trials). On the other hand, in Israel the discussion of the legality and the implementation of the death penalty were more prevalent.

Responsibility For the Crimes

How did the newspapers in the study view guilt and responsibility for the Holocaust and the Nazi crimes? What knowledge was implied and what reactions to it were claimed? Table 27 presents the varied expressions on these matters as they appeared in newspaper statements.

Such statements, too, were made more than twice as often in the Israeli press (n = 1,258) as in the German press (n = 476). However, due to the limited number of cases, especially in some of the trials, certain individual statements rarely appeared. The largest absolute number (n = 217) appeared during the Nuremberg trial; there were almost as many statements during the Eichmann trial (n = 212), far fewer during the Auschwitz trial (n = 47), and not a single statement about responsibility for the Holocaust during the Demjanjuk trial.

The notion of collective guilt was most often mentioned in the coverage by the German newspapers, particularly during the Auschwitz trial. Also, knowledge of the crimes by Germans was accepted rather than disputed or held to be uncertain. Only knowledge of the total extent of the crimes was claimed to be unknown. Finally, it was stated relatively often—especially during the Eichmann and Auschwitz trials— that there were Germans who aided persecuted people.

The largest number of statements concerning responsibility for the Holocaust was made in the Israeli press during the Eichmann trial (n = 825) and the smallest number during the Demjanjuk trial (n = 60). Substantially more than in Germany, Israeli newspapers explicitly stated that the Germans were responsible for the consequences of National Socialism. In Israel, as in Germany, collective guilt of the Germans was mentioned relatively often, more than most of the other theses, and here, too, it was more often implied than rejected. Moreover, in the Israeli newspapers not only were Germans claimed to have had knowledge of the crimes but to an even larger extent so was the Western world and to a lesser degree so were the Jews living in Palestine. In contrast, in the Israeli press there was distinctly less talk about the help given by Germans to persecuted people, except during the Auschwitz trial.

Table 27. Statements Regarding Responsibility for Crimes (in Percent).

	GERMAN NEWSPAPERS				
	Nuremberg Trial $n = 217$	Eichmann Trial $n = 212$	Auschwitz Trial $n = 47$	Demjanjuk Trial $n = 0$	Total $n = 476$
Collective guilt	19	15	26	-	18
Demand for collective guilt	5	1	-	-	3
Rejection of collective guilt	5	7	9	-	6
No demand for collective guilt	12	2	2	-	7
Collective shame	3	8	-	-	5
Demand for collective shame	-	3	2	-	2
Rejection of collective shame	-	-	2	-	-
No demand for collective shame	-	-	-	-	-
Germans knew of persecution	20	7	11	-	13
Doubt Germans knew of persecution	10	4	9	-	7
Germans did not know of persecution	2	-	-	-	1
Germans knew of extent of persecution	1	2	-	-	2
Doubt Germans knew extent	7	5	6	-	6
Germans didn't know extent	-	-	2	-	-
Some help received from Germans	4	22	26	-	14
No help received from Germans	-	-	4	-	1
Germans responsible for consequences	3	8	-	-	5

Table 27. Statements Regarding Responsibility for Crimes (in Percent). (con't)

	Nuremberg Trial n = 200	ISRAELI NEWSPAPERS Eichmann Trial n = 825	ISRAELI NEWSPAPERS Auschwitz Trial n = 173	ISRAELI NEWSPAPERS Demjanjuk Trial n = 60	Total n = 1258
Germans not responsible	–	5	–	–	2
Jews in Palestine knew of persecution	–	–	–	–	–
Jews in Palestine didn't know	–	–	–	–	–
Doubt Jews knew of persecution	–	–	–	–	–
People in West knew of persecution	4	2	2	–	3
People in West didn't know	–	–	–	–	–
Doubt people in West knew	–	–	–	–	–
Other	2	7	–	–	4
Total	97	98	101	–	99
Collective guilt	17	13	6	17	13
Demand for collective guilt	1	3	6	13	4
Rejection of collective guilt	5	4	6	–	4
No demand for collective guilt	1	2	3	2	2
Collective shame	2	2	1	–	2
Demand for collective shame	1	1	3	2	1
Rejection of collective shame	–	–	–	2	1
No demand for collective shame	–	–	2	2	1
Germans knew of persecution	4	6	6	3	6

Table 27. Statements Regarding Responsibility for Crimes (in Percent). (con't)

Doubt Germans knew of persecution	1	1	1	-	1
Germans did not know of persecution	1	-	1	-	-
Germans knew of extent of persecution	4	6	3	2	5
Doubt Germans knew extent	5	2	2	-	3
Germans didn't know extent	1	1	1	-	1
Some help received from Germans	5	6	15	7	7
No help received from Germans	1	1	1	2	1
Germans responsible for consequences	15	15	20	30	17
Germans not responsible	1	6	5	-	4
Jews in Palestine knew of persecution	1	3	-	2	2
Jews in Palestine didn't know	-	1	-	2	1
Doubt Jews knew of persecution	1	-	1	-	-
People in West knew of persecution	3	11	3	7	9
People in West didn't know	1	1	-	-	1
Doubt people in West knew	1	1	-	-	1
Other	30	14	11	10	16
Total	102	100	98	103	103

Causes of the Holocaust

As can be seen in Table 28, statements about the possible causes that led to the seizure of power by the Nazis in Germany and thereby, eventually, to the Holocaust, were infrequently made in either the German newspapers (n = 124) or the Israeli newspapers (n = 241). The major cause of the Holocaust in both countries was anti-Semitism (27% in Israel and 19% in Germany). In Germany, of equal importance was the German national character, whereas in Israel relatively many items mentioned Jewish characteristics. Historic, political, and economic causes were less frequently cited in both countries.

Anti-Semitism

It is noteworthy that there were nearly eight times as many statements about anti-Semitism in the Israeli coverage of the trials (n = 353) than in the German coverage (n = 46). As Table 29 indicates, in both countries the coverage of anti-Semitism was treated not just as an historical fact but mainly as a current phenomenon. The fact that anti-Semitism was so infrequently dealt with in the German newspapers during the Nuremberg and Eichmann trials and not at all during the Auschwitz and Demjanjuk trials should be particularly noteworthy.

Evaluation of the Verdicts

The last statement category dealt with is how the four trial verdicts were assessed in the newspapers (see Table 30). Despite the different extent of the coverage in both countries, the total number of statements dealing with the verdicts was the same, although they were distributed differently among the individual trials.

In Germany over 70% of such evaluations came from items about the Nuremberg trial; thus these verdicts obviously presented the greatest opportunity for statements of opinion. Given the fact that the claim that the sentences were too light was overwhelming, it could have been applicable to cases in which prison sentences or acquittals were pronounced, as many of the defendants in the Nuremberg trial received death sentences. During the Eichmann trial the most frequent argument (64%) was that no appropriate sentence was possible, whereas in the case of the Auschwitz trial 50% of the statements claimed that the sentence was too light (caution should be taken in interpreting these percentages given the small number of cases).

Table 28. Statements Regarding Causes of the Holocaust (in Percent).

	GERMAN NEWSPAPERS				
	Nuremberg Trial $n = 54$	Eichmann Trial $n = 52$	Auschwitz Trial $n = 18$	Demjanjuk Trial $n = 0$	Total $n = 124$
Historic reasons	13	8	17	-	11
German characteristics	24	19	6	-	19
Jewish characteristics	-	2	6	-	2
Loss of religious ties	11	12	11	-	11
Decay of political order	17	4	28	-	13
Economic situation	9	4	6	-	6
Cultural decline	7	13	6	-	10
Anti-Semitism	7	35	11	-	19
Other	11	4	11	-	8
Total	99	101	102	-	99

Table 28. Statements Regarding Causes of the Holocaust (in Percent). (con't)

			ISRAELI NEWSPAPERS		
	Nuremberg Trial n = 64	Eichmann Trial n = 131	Auschwitz Trial n = 28	Demjanjuk Trial n = 18	Total n = 241
Historic reasons	5	8	7	6	7
German characteristics	5	8	11	-	7
Jewish characteristics	17	18	43	11	20
Loss of religious ties	17	11	4	6	11
Decay of political order	-	4	-	-	2
Economic situation	2	2	7	11	3
Cultural decline	5	5	-	6	5
Anti-Semitism	25	26	18	50	27
Other	25	18	11	11	19
Total	101	100	101	101	101

Table 29. Statements Regarding Anti-Semitism (in Percent).

GERMAN NEWSPAPERS

	Nuremberg Trial n = 9	Eichmann Trial n = 37	Auschwitz Trial n = 0	Demjanjuk Trial n = 0	Total n = 46
Historical phenomenon	44	32	-	-	35
Current problem	22	54	-	-	49
Both	22	8	-	-	11
Other	11	5	-	-	6
Total	99	99	-	-	101

ISRAELI NEWSPAPERS

	Nuremberg Trial n = 59	Eichmann Trial n = 227	Auschwitz Trial n = 29	Demjanjuk Trial n = 38	Total n = 353
Historic phenomenon	37	19	31	29	24
Current problem	17	48	24	37	40
Both	39	32	38	34	34
Other	7	2	7	-	3
Total	100	101	100	100	101

Table 30. Statements Regarding Evaluations of the Verdicts (in Percent).

	Nuremberg Trial n = 231	Eichmann Trial n = 14	Auschwitz Trial n = 46	Demjanjuk Trial n = 6	Total n = 297
			GERMAN NEWSPAPERS		
Appropriate	18	36	28	50	21
Punishment too severe	10	-	-	17	8
Punishment too light	71	64	50	-	64
No proper punishment possible	1	-	20	17	7
Other	-	-	2	17	1
Total	100	100	100	101	101

	Nuremberg Trial n = 42	Eichmann Trial n = 143	Auschwitz Trial n = 51	Demjanjuk Trial n = 62	Total n = 298
			ISRAELI NEWSPAPERS		
Appropriate	12	50	10	48	37
Punishment too severe	5	13	16	19	13
Punishment too light	43	3	53	2	17
No proper punishment possible	10	17	18	15	16
Other	31	17	4	16	16
Total	101	100	101	100	99

Whereas the German newspapers did not overwhelmingly claim that the verdicts in the trials that took place in Germany were appropriate, the Israeli newspapers by and large supported the verdicts of the trials that took place in Israel. In the Israeli newspapers the largest number of evaluations of the verdict were made regarding the Eichmann trial ($n = 143$), with half of the statements declaring the verdict to be just. The Demjanjuk trial produced similar results. On the other hand, regarding the trials conducted in Germany, the preponderance of opinion was that the punishments imposed by the German courts were too light. Once again, these opinions must have reflected the points of view of the victims, whose immeasurable suffering had been caused by the defendants.

METAPHORS AND LOADED TERMS

Journalistic writing is generally not flowery and metaphoric. The coverage of certain events, however, lends itself to the use of different language, including the use of metaphors. As Table 31 indicates, the use of metaphors was noticeably greater in the Israeli newspapers (699 items containing a metaphor) compared with the German press (166 items). This suggests a different framing of Holocaust events in the two countries. Metaphors are used to help coping with terrible events when conventional language does not suffice. They also may create myths through which historical events are placed within overarching contexts. Thus myths relating to the Holocaust must have been closer and more relevant to Israeli perceptions than to the German mind.

Several kinds of metaphors were used. First, Nazi perpetrators were compared in both countries to monsters or animals, thereby characterizing their inhumanity. A common expression in Israel, especially during the Eichmann trial, was that the Jews "were led like sheep to the slaughter" which became a standard mantra in Israel, evoking the unresisting surrender with which the Jews submitted to mass annihilation. The expression comes from the Old Testament (Isaiah 53:7 and Jeremiah 11:19) and therefore possesses a particularly mythic connection. In Germany this metaphor was quoted only occasionally during the Eichmann trial.

In Israel other comparisons to Old Testament events were also suggested, whereas in the German press, at least during the Nuremberg and Eichmann trials, additional metaphoric (and, by implication, Christian) references to the New Testament slipped in. Reporters in Israel occasionally resorted to apocalyptic metaphors, made comparisons to historical barbarians and monsters (Attila the Hun and Genghis

Table 31. Use of Metaphors in Items (in Percent).

	GERMAN NEWSPAPERS				
	Nuremberg Trial n = 37	Eichmann Trial n = 61	Auschwitz Trial n = 65	Demjanjuk Trial n = 3	Total n = 166
"Like sheep to the slaughter"	-	2	-	-	1
Old Testament	3	8	14	-	9
New Testament	8	13	-	-	7
Monsters	49	10	9	67	19
Animals	24	25	20	-	22
Other	16	43	57	33	42
Total	100	101	100	100	100

	ISRAELI NEWSPAPERS				
	Nuremberg Trial n = 36	Eichmann Trial n = 443	Auschwitz Trial n = 96	Demjanjuk Trial n = 124	Total n = 699
"Like sheep to the slaughter"	3	14	5	11	12
Old Testament	6	15	8	15	13
New Testament	6	3	2	2	3
Monsters	8	33	16	35	30
Animals	50	33	34	23	35
Other	28	3	34	13	10
Total	101	101	99	99	103

Khan), spoke of "Hell" and "slaughterhouses," and referred to organized mass murder (death machine, machinery of annihilation). Such
metaphorical wrappings allowed not only for uncommon linguistic
usage and journalistic style to be recognized, but also a spiritual and fig-
urative emotional frame of reference with which people (especially in
Israel) could try to come to terms with the experiences of the Holocaust.

In addition to metaphors, an attempt was also made in the content analysis to examine the terminology used in the newspapers to
describe the crimes committed against the Jews. Eight such terms were
identified in the newspaper items (Table 32). It should be noted that in
the table no total percentages are provided because the coding was done
separately for each of the eight terms, as dichotomous variables, and the
data in the table reflect the presence for each term. Furthermore, any
given item could contain more than one term.

In general these terms were used more frequently by the Israeli
press than by the German newspapers. It is most striking that the famil-
iar term "Holocaust," which by the time the trials were being conducted
was in general use, even in Germany, didn't appear at all in the German
newspaper coverage of the first three trials until the Demjanjuk trial,
when it first appeared. Indeed, as Frei (1992) remarked, there existed for
a long time in the Federal Republic of Germany a "termless" phrase with
regard to the crimes committed against Jews. This evidently changed
from 1979 onwards following the broadcast of the American television
mini-series *Holocaust*. The dramatic series popularized the term and ever
since it has been commonly accepted in Germany. The series also helped
in making the term a "household word" in America and in other countries where it was aired (Shandler, 1999).

It should be noted that the term *Holocaust* is an English word of
ancient origin, a translation of the biblical Hebrew term *Shoa*, both of
which refer to a sacrifice or destruction, usually by fire. Whereas *Shoa*
was adopted in Israel and *Holocaust* was adopted in America as the
"official" modern term for the events of World War II, no equivalent
term was coined in most other countries or languages, including
Germany.

Thus in Israel, the Hebrew term *Shoa* had come into common
use much earlier and was already present in the coverage of the
Nuremberg trial. During the Eichmann trial it showed up on average in
every fourth newspaper item. It appeared less frequently during the
Auschwitz trial, perhaps because that trial took place in Germany
where, as noted, the term was not yet in use, presumably also during the
trial proceedings. During the Demjanjuk trial it could again be found in
approximately every fifth report.

Table 32. Use of Loaded Terms in Items (in Percent).

GERMAN NEWSPAPERS

	Nuremberg Trial n = 1722	Eichmann Trial n = 784	Auschwitz Trial n = 931	Demjanjuk Trial n = 111	Total n = 3548
Holocaust	-	-	-	10	-
Race	7	5	4	-	5
Anti-Semitism	5	12	1	3	5
Martyrdom	1	-	-	-	1
Heroism	-	-	-	-	-
Genocide	1	3	-	3	2
Extermination	14	26	12	5	16
Pogrom	4	1	-	1	2

ISRAELI NEWSPAPERS

	Nuremberg Trial n = 797	Eichmann Trial n = 3118	Auschwitz Trial n = 558	Demjanjuk Trial n = 1199	Total n = 5672
Holocaust	3	26	6	19	19
Race	5	7	2	2	5
Anti-Semitism	8	9	4	3	7
Martyrdom	-	1	-	-	1
Heroism	1	5	4	1	4
Genocide	4	8	9	3	6
Extermination	21	40	47	26	35
Pogrom	5	2	1	1	2

However, in Israel (as in Germany) the coverage most often spoke less specifically by referring to the "extermination" of the Jews. The term "genocide" was also less frequently used in Israel, but nevertheless more so than in Germany. And again, the perspective of the victims was emphasized when their behavior during the Holocaust was at times—although not often—referred to in the Israeli press as "heroic," which did not occur in the German press.

EMOTIONAL TONE OF THE ITEMS

In view of the nature of the crimes being reported it must have been difficult for the journalists to maintain an objective and temperate tone in the coverage of the trials. Thus a more-than-usual amount of emotionalism could have been expected. This was examined both in the headlines and in the text of the items.

As for the headlines, more were classified as emotional in Germany (19%) than in Israel (only 6% of all headlines). In both countries the relatively most frequent emotional headlines were during the Auschwitz trial (33% in the German newspapers and 11% in the Israeli newspapers).

As for the emotional content of the items themselves, Table 33 presents the data, which stand in bold contrast to that of the headlines. An attempt was made to distinguish between low emotional content and high emotional content. Whereas in Germany, on average, 68% of the items were judged by the coders to be neutral, that is, lacking any emotion, in Israel only 52% of the items were coded as being neutral. In both countries slightly over one quarter of the items were coded as being of low emotion.

The coverage in both countries differed mainly in relation to the items with a high emotional content. The coders were under the impression that in Israel, on average, 22% of the items exhibited such content, whereas only 5% of the items were so coded in Germany. In Israel, this was most poignantly the case during the Eichmann and Auschwitz trials, and least so during the Nuremberg trial. In Germany, too, the largest proportion of highly emotional items concerned the Auschwitz trial, although to a lesser degree than in Israel. The main reason for this must have been, as has been established, that during the Auschwitz trial the description of cruelties piled up.

Table 33. Emotional Content of Items (in Percent).

GERMAN NEWSPAPERS

	Nuremberg Trial n = 1722	Eichmann Trial n = 784	Auschwitz Trial n = 931	Demjanjuk Trial n = 111	Total n = 3548
Low	33	38	16	70	31
Neutral	77	73	45	81	68
Low emotional content	19	23	47	17	27
High emotional content	4	5	8	2	5
Total	100	101	100	100	100

ISRAELI NEWSPAPERS

	Nuremberg Trial n = 787	Eichmann Trial n = 3107	Auschwitz Trial n = 555	Demjanjuk Trial n = 1188	Total n = 5637
Neutral	56	48	46	56	52
Low emotional content	24	25	30	27	26
High emotional content	19	27	24	17	22
Total	99	100	100	100	100

6

Dissociation and Identification

In Chapter Three it was suggested that several stages exist both in Germany and in Israel in terms of how the two societies dealt with the Holocaust and with the Nazi era. Following the presentation of the data on the coverage of the four trials, the question becomes what light, if any does the current analysis shed on the stages outlined earlier. Is the existence of such stages confirmed by the analysis of the newspapers or do the data reveal a different picture?

The number and the extent of the newspaper items indisputably show that considerable information was presented in the press in both countries. The German data have shown that a great deal of newspaper space was devoted to the Nuremberg trial in 1945-46. Indeed, the reporting of the Nuremberg trial in Germany was the most thorough of all four trials (particularly when considered in relation to the size of the newspapers). Of course it should be recalled that the reporting of the Nuremberg trial was "prescribed" as part of the Allied Occupying Powers' re-education project. Thus the willingness to provide full coverage of the trial didn't necessarily emanate directly from the German reporters' own initiative or from a desire for full clarification on the part of the German public. That does not mean, however, that these were entirely lacking. Furthermore, this issue is of secondary importance if one is interested in focusing on what information about the Nazi past became available to the public by way of newspaper reporting of the trial.

An attempt was made by the German newspapers to use an appropriate graphic layout to help overcome the selection threshold and the readers' putative desire not to know. To this end other available media were also used, including the "The World in Film" newsreel put out by the American and British Allies. This series alone showed 23 filmed reports during the course of the Nuremberg trial. Thus in view of this and the newspapers examined in the study it can hardly be maintained that the Nuremberg trial found "little expression . . . in contemporary public life" (Steinbach, 1981, p. 43) or to quote Lübbe (1985, p. 52) that the "intensity of the occupation with National Socialism, to the extent that it can be measured by the amount of public . . . expression, was rather slight in the first years after the collapse of National Socialism." One must rather acknowledge that there is no reason to "concede that there was a waiting period immediately after the war in the German's awareness of the Holocaust" (Rosen, 1985, p. 62).

In Israel more attention was accorded to the Nuremberg trial than to the Auschwitz trial, but less than to the other two trials conducted in Jerusalem. And yet, the scope of what was reported seems to contradict the thesis of a far-reaching silence about the Holocaust in Israel as well. It is, of course, true that the reporting was far less extensive, that it consisted of relatively short items, and that it was less prominently displayed than in Germany. However, the modest nature of the pre-State Israeli newspapers at that time must be taken into account, especially with regard to the Nuremberg trial. The focal point of the Nuremberg trial, based on the indictments—and consequently the focus of the newspaper reporting as well—was not yet fixated on the annihilation of the Jews. Other war crimes that were before the court took priority. However, the Jewish press in Palestine already gave more weight to the murder of Jews than did the German press, which instead featured the preparation for and the waging of war, as they appeared in the indictments.

The breakthrough in public perception of the Holocaust in Israel occurred during the Eichmann trial and was unequivocally confirmed by the findings of the current content analysis. None of the other Nazi trials were subject to so much reporting, neither in Israel itself nor—to an even greater degree—in Germany. The urgency with which people in Israel followed the trial proceedings against one of the people chiefly responsible for the "final solution to the Jewish problem" found expression both in the flood of articles and in the way they were presented. In this trial—in contrast to the Nuremberg trial—the fate of the Jews was clearly the central point of both the judicial and extrajudicial attention. At the same time the events of the trial stimulated both a journalistic and a social examination of other narrowly defined nonjudicial aspects of the

Holocaust. Thus, from a thematic point of view, the reporting of the Eichmann trial was less limited to the trial itself than was the reporting of the other three trials. This, again, corresponded to the political intention closely connected with the trial in Israel, namely the attempt to elucidate the "over-all experience" of the Holocaust.

This was similar in Germany, not in its extent, but from a thematic perspective. Indeed, due to editorial decisions taken during the Eichmann trial less was reported compared with the Nuremberg trial or with the coverage that the trial had received in Israel. However, there were still a considerable number of items. The fact that the German newspapers temporarily sent their own correspondents to Jerusalem substantiates their perceived importance of this trial. The German journalists made sure that their newspapers likewise not only covered the progress of the trial, to a large extent from the journalists' own perspectives, but also that questions reaching beyond the trial were brought up. Thus in the other three trials the German press, for example, hardly dealt with moral aspects or public responses to the facts of the case.

Considering the voluminous attention given to the Eichmann trial in the German newspapers, it is surprising to encounter time and again the view in contemporary historical literature to the effect that the Auschwitz trial was the first in the Federal Republic to actually examine the Nazi era in detail, including the mass murder of Jews (Steinbach, 1981). There is no doubt, as the content analysis indicates, that more was reported in Germany about the Auschwitz trial than about the Eichmann trial. However, this was above all due to the trial's long duration and to the fact that it took place domestically, in close proximity to the events discussed in the trial, therefore promoting constant attention. It is also possible that during the Eichmann trial the public was not yet ready to cope with the full significance of the Holocaust. In this sense, the press coverage of the Eichmann trial may have preceded its time but in retrospect can be seen as having set the stage for the Auschwitz trial, which followed soon after and thus enabled the press to delve into more details in its examination of what took place.

One reason for the perception of a change in consciousness may lie in the peculiarities of the Auschwitz trial. The issue under contention was not the "over-all experience" of the Holocaust, and no single person responsible for the organization of his department was on trial. Instead, those standing trial were people who implemented the daily execution and annihilation of Jews in the concentration and death camps. This no longer allowed for a defense option of self-exoneration that was possible in trials of "chief offenders." This was reflected in the contents of the reporting about the Auschwitz trial in which, for example, the atrocities committed against Jews were described in more detail than in the other cases.

In Israel, interest in the Auschwitz trial lagged far behind interest in the Eichmann trial. Occurring two years later, the Auschwitz trial was entirely in the shadow of that of Eichmann. Thus the reporting was not only much less extensive, but also quite discontinuous. Again, the location and the duration of the trial would have been the decisive factors. As the trial took place in Frankfurt before a German court, it had less meaning for an internal Israeli examination of the Holocaust. After the "great event" of the Eichmann trial, of which the public in Israel felt to a certain degree that it had had enough, the Auschwitz trial was no longer so newsworthy. Another reason for the relatively low coverage of the trial in Israel was the fact that it was conducted as a normal criminal proceeding. This meant that every detail had to be substantiated and proven with regard to its date, time, and precise location. This process became quite tedious for the public to follow on a daily basis. In addition, two major Nazi criminals associated with Auschwitz—Rudolph Höss, the camp commander, and Yosef Mengele, the notorious doctor who experimented on inmates—were not being tried (the former was found guilty and executed in a separate trial and the latter escaped and was never found). This might have caused some diminished interest in the trial.

And yet, because the testimony presented in the trial did describe the cruelty suffered by the victims, the trial was nonetheless guaranteed a presence in the Israeli press as well. Israelis were also particularly interested in the reactions of the German public to the trial, even more than during the Eichmann trial.

The actual reporting and its public perception in both countries differ most strongly with regard to the last trial in the study, in which the denationalized United States citizen John Demjanjuk stood accused. Four decades after the end of the war and two decades after the Auschwitz trial, the proceedings taking place before an Israeli court received only marginal notice in the German press. Of course, the case was indeed reported, but the space allotted to it was far less than that devoted to the earlier trials. By and large, only sporadic items appeared, mainly at the beginning and at the end of the proceedings. Little was communicated in detail about the course of the trial. Procedural aspects were the focus of the reporting more than usual, especially the dominant question of the defendant's identity. The limited interest in the trial might have been due, among other things, to the fact that the accused was a native Ukrainian, not a German. This might have negatively affected German interest in the reporting of the trial and justified its modest scope. In addition, it must also be seen as an indication of "historicizing" the Holocaust, due to the increased temporal distance from the events and to the change in generations in Germany.

The situation was quite different in Israel. To a certain extent the Demjanjuk trial represented an attempt to create a new edition of the Eichmann trial, with the decided intention of once again using a Nazi trial as a catalyst for shaping Israeli identity and providing another generation with a profound experience of the Holocaust. The trial and through it the Holocaust itself were once again instrumentalized for internal political purposes. These significant issues found expression in correspondingly intensive reporting. Surely, the reporting did not match the scope of the Eichmann trial, but it did surpass it in certain ways—especially the use of illustrations—that were likely to have drawn attention to it. Instead of historicizing, this was rather a case of actualizing the Holocaust that was at the same time part of that "paradoxical process of mythification" of which Zimmermann (1992) speaks. The Israeli press focused on the procedural aspects of the trial but the multithematization that typified its press coverage of the Eichmann trial did not occur in the Israeli coverage of the Demjanjuk trial.

The differences between the press coverage of the trials in Germany and in Israel were generally greater than the differences among the various newspapers in each of the two countries. Political differences based on affiliation that would normally be found in the press with regard to other topics were minimized or at least did not blatantly appear in reports on the trials. This does not mean, however, that no individual differences existed in certain instances.

A fundamental difference that has been repeatedly stressed is that in Germany the reporting was more strongly oriented towards the defendants whereas in Israel, by comparison, it was more about the victims. Not that the defendants' point of view in the German press was condoned or that they were spared or exonerated, but the reporting was certainly characterized by questions of who the offenders were and what they had done. In Israel, on the other hand, people were naturally on the side of the victims and sympathized with their suffering. This offender versus victim perspective in both countries determined the respective "framing" in the depictions of the Holocaust. The current study confirms at every step how profound this difference was and it can hardly be overlooked. It is interesting to note how Ruth Klüger (1992), in her memoir *Weiter leben*, commented about this:

> Moreover, it occurs to me that the questions that Germans discussed in such conversations (about the Holocaust) revolved around the offenders, while the Jews wanted to know more about the victims. Nothing about the victims occurred to Germans other than that they just passively gave up. We, on the other hand, tugged and pulled at them, at the murdered people, wanting them to identify themselves or justify us in our actions and lack of them. (p. 96)

This essential difference is expressed in detail in numerous examples in the press of the two countries. They include formal and content differences. In the Israeli press there was more discussion of the extermination of Jews, more emphasis on the survivors and their present condition, the atrocities were mentioned more often and in greater detail, and questions of morality were more prevalent. Additional issues raised more frequently in the Israeli press were lessons to be learned from the Holocaust, responsibility for the Holocaust, and the figure of six million victims. Regarding photographs, in Israel the focus was on witnesses—mostly survivors—and there were more scenes of the concentration camps. Finally, more metaphors appeared in the Israeli press. In Germany, on the other hand, there was more mention of the extermination of non-Jews as well as the characteristics and personality of the accused. Likewise, the photographs focused more on the defendants.

The findings of the present study can be considered principally from two perspectives: that of a contemporary analysis of events and that of the role of journalism. From the former, which has already been discussed, the reporting in the newspapers can be viewed as a public expression and one of the means for "assimilating" the Holocaust and the Nazi era in the two countries. As for the journalism-communication perspective, different questions arise. Similarities and differences in reporting reflect, among other things, criteria of framing strategies and selection. In both countries "proximity" and "shock and dismay" were perhaps definitive as factors in reporting the news. They explain, for example, the different weight given to the four trials in the press and also stipulate the focus on the accused or the victims.

The long duration of the Nazi trials examined must have been especially problematic from a reporting point of view. Journalists ordinarily prefer short-term events, and when possible those that begin and end within the publication cycle of the medium (day, week, month, etc.). This time frame was never the case with regard to the Nazi war crimes trials. As Dietrich Strothmann (1984), who covered the Auschwitz trial for the German weekly *Die Zeit*, remarked self-critically about the consequences of journalistic reporting:

> As a rule, I only wrote about the trial when I knew, on the basis of prior information, that there was going to be an "interesting day." It might be that notable witnesses were testifying, or that unusual facts of the case would be discussed that day. In this event I was most likely to go. (p. 114)

The rules of journalistic attention and selection are actually in opposition to the steady attention required by events such as the Nazi war crimes trials. These rules determined the course of the reporting and were decisive with regard to fluctuations and discontinuities. On the other hand, the notion of what is newsworthy is expanded as a result of the willingness to report continuously, once the selection threshold has been overcome. In the case of the press coverage of the trials analyzed in this study, the fact that the prolonged trials had "natural" high points played into the hands of the journalists making it possible for them to keep coming back to the trials even after periods of relative disinterest. This ultimately led to a considerable degree of continuity in reporting on the four Nazi trials, although the treatment of the Demjanjuk trial in the German press was an exception.

The influence of journalists on the depiction of the Holocaust and the Nazi era in the context of the trial reporting is not only manifested in the selection of information to be communicated and the resulting formation of attitudes. It can also be found in the commentary and evaluation, not only their own, but also that of other authors and sources. Many such statements related predominantly to the personality of the defendants and to their character as well as to the course of the trial proceedings themselves. Sometimes in one instance there might be a reference to the defendant and in another, a critical evaluation of the legality of the proceedings. In short, the specific problematic content of the Nazi trials—their legal base, the jurisdiction of the court, the credibility of the witnesses, the responsibility of the accused, and so forth—were in no way played down, neither in the German press nor in the Israeli.

Finally, how should the newspaper reporting be evaluated in terms of its depiction of the Holocaust and of the Nazi era? An answer to this question, which in view of the conclusions of the present study is unavoidable, depends on one's expectations, standards, and demands. This is especially true for all judgments about "overcoming the past." The higher one sets the normative moral demands, the more critical the judgment. How contrary these positions can be was evident until recently in the Federal Republic of (West) Germany. Giordano (1987), an exponent of one position, has pointedly spoken of a "second guilt" that the Germans incurred through repression and denial, following the first one under Hitler. Kittel (1993), an exponent of the other position, referred to the thesis of a second guilt as a "legend" and pointed to many occasions and ways in which people concerned themselves with the Nazi past as early as in Chancellor Adenauer's era in the 1950s. The chasm between the two positions can be partly explained empirically if it can be demonstrated that representatives of both positions base them on different reference points and events. However, the gap can be explained much better as a result of different interpretations stemming from the fundamental assessment criteria in which political positions play a part.

Based on the findings of the study, the extent to which the four trials were covered tends to contradict the repression thesis, or at least there is hardly any evidence to support it. Whatever agenda setting the press created can be all too easily overlooked in hindsight. Looking at the combined data for the four trials, the Israeli coverage was more extensive. However, this was a result of the particularly heavy coverage of the Eichmann and Demjanjuk trials in Israel. It cannot be denied that the initial position for the study of the trials in Germany—the land of the offenders—must have been quite different from that in Israel—the land of the victims. This would have produced different motives for agenda setting as well as for temporary suppression. Moreover, in Israel there was likewise controversy about the Holocaust and its social significance.

Having found in the content analysis that there was no lack of elucidation about the Nazi trials in the press, this does not mean that there were no insufficiencies. Certain elements do seem to have been entirely absent or at least underrepresented, especially in the German newspapers. And yet, it is important to consider the fact that in both countries the press generally followed the latest developments in the trials, a fact that restricted certain angles of potential coverage.

For example, weren't the causes and the origins of the Holocaust, which led to the terrible crimes, featured less than they might have been? Or weren't there too few reflections about the lessons to be drawn from the events? It is striking, for example, that compared with the Israeli reporting, anti-Semitism hardly showed up in the German newspapers. Anti-Semitism was neither cited sufficiently as a cause of the Holocaust (although the term could certainly be found) nor was there a connection drawn from it to the continuing contemporary phenomenon. Perhaps something of the taboo-like nature of dealing with anti-Semitism and the simultaneous moralizing about which Bergmann and Erb (1991) spoke of in their study of the German postwar period could once again be found.

Moreover, even if attention to and "empathy" for the victims was not lacking in the German newspapers, isn't this still additional proof of the "fading out of the history of the victims" in Germany of which Frei (1992) spoke? Isn't it too simplistic to put the accused so much into the foreground, thereby creating targets whose guilt could divert attention from collective responsibility? Responsibility for the consequences of the Holocaust was, as has been established in the current data, a more dominant theme in Israel than in Germany. On the other hand, knowledge of the people living at the time who knew about the crimes was assumed to be greater in Germany than in Israel. As Bergmann and Erb (1990) put it:

Israel and the Jews regard Germany through the spectacles of the
past, but the Germans see themselves through the spectacles of the
present and the future and would rather avoid looking into the past,
especially the recent past (the clean break tendency). (p. 15)

This may be altogether correct; certainly the statement is confirmed by many of the findings of the present study. But opposite tendencies show up as well. The Israeli press reported on the interest of the
German public in the trial proceedings more than the German press did.
And the Israeli press showed interest in current issues in other ways as
well. All these add up to the impression that the proceedings were treated in Germany in a rather isolated manner, merely as criminal trials,
whereas in Israel—through a more diverse and graphic portrayal—they
were presented as more strongly tied to current social processes.

Nonetheless, the extent and continuity of the reporting in
Germany about the Nuremberg, Eichmann, and Auschwitz trials was
considerable and it can be assumed that in any case it created public
attention to Nazi crimes and made the readers "witnesses" to what had
occurred. Even if lessons from the Holocaust were hardly mentioned in
the coverage, this does not mean that the reporting on the whole was not
instrumentalized, for the journalists charged themselves with the task of
elucidating beyond what was required by the anticipated public interest.
The following quotation from Steinbach (1981) acknowledges the controversial aspect of this journalistic self-awareness:

In the matter of Nazi crimes many journalists bucked public opinion, they did not practice complaisant journalism and reproached all
those lies that denied the ability of journalism to want to or be able
to communicate insights and attitudes. The media played a leading
part in the discussion of the Nazi trials and turned against the tendency to leave the problem alone, not to mention responsibilities, to
sweep guilt under the carpet. (p. 37)

The analysis of the reporting of the Nazi trials can indeed be
interpreted as a social phenomenon inasmuch as it deals with the Nazi
era and the Holocaust. This does not mean, however, that direct infer-
ences may be drawn from the analysis of the newspaper contents to the
actual "processing" of the information by readers and its consequences
for opinion formation and change. This is probably the case even for so
sensitive a topic as the Nazi trials, whose depiction must of necessity
have brought many Germans into a state of cognitive dissonance. And
yet, efforts at understanding were also not likely to be totally ineffectual
even if the press may not have—for media-specific dramaturgical reasons—triggered so strong an upheaval as, for example, the 1979 broad-

cast of the television series *Holocaust*. It remains to be seen—if it is at all methodologically possible—whether the one-time showing of the television series will ultimately have proven to be more effective than the newspaper reporting about the trials that went on for years.

Only flimsy arguments can dispute the fact that there were lasting effects in the Federal Republic from its preoccupation with the Nazi past and the Holocaust. Such effects can still be seen when comparing the West German situation to that of the former (East) German Democratic Republic. It is not only that the basic premises were different in the East because the offenders had mainly fled to the West. The communist regime made it far more a point to deny the collective German responsibility for the Nazi era (Grabitz, 1994; Wieland, 1991). There was absolutely no discussion of complicity. The first comparative population surveys, conducted in 1990 following the political changes and the reunification of East and West Germany, provided some interesting findings. Thus, for example, in an August 1992 survey (Institut für Demoskopie, 1992), in reply to the question "What do you think is most special about our history, what distinguishes our history from that of other countries?" 52% of West Germans mentioned the Third Reich, National Socialism, or Hitler and 17% made specific references to Nazi crimes and the annihilation of the Jews. In contrast, only 11% of the former East German sample mentioned the Third Reich as something special about German history and only 4% mentioned Nazi crimes. These data clearly show that National Socialism and the Holocaust were much more omnipresent in the national history of the West German population than of the East German population. This gap in consciousness can indeed be attributed to different agendas set in the mass media of the former two Germanys.

The Holocaust and its "processing" had a fundamentally different function in Israel than in Germany during the post-war years. The Israeli media, along with the country's educational system, played an important role in defining this function, which significantly influenced the awareness and the perception of the Holocaust in Israel (Zimmermann, 1992). In the meantime, however, there were growing voices claiming that the popular instrumentalization of the Holocaust had become problematic. Zimmermann even claimed that attempts at elucidation in recent times—in the mythifying phase—has been carried on *ad absurdum*. In this context the staging of the Demjanjuk trial was specifically cited as an example of the downright "obsessive preoccupation with the Holocaust." Zimmermann sees in this process the danger of a "boomerang effect" that alienates Israeli society from mastering its current problems. Therefore in Israel the mythification was accompanied by a de-historicizing of the Holocaust, so that the term also became a formula applicable to entirely different historical facts such as, for example, the threat to Israelis posed by terrorists, Palestinians, or Arabs (Nossek, 1994). Last but not least the Israeli war experience (the Six-Day War, the Yom Kippur War and the Gulf War) caused Israelis to feel threatened and isolated, feelings that brought the Holocaust to mind and strengthened the desire to keep the country strong.

In an overall sense, the reporting about the Holocaust, which was examined in the present study of the four Nazi trials, lies in an area of tension between what Elias (1983) refers to as "identification" (*Aneignung*) and "dissociation" (*Abwehr*). Elias coined these two concepts in the context of social research but does not refer to "two independent human tendencies." He rather refers to archetypes defining a continuum of:

> shifting balances between two types of behavioral and experiential impulses [that] . . . push one now more towards identification and now more towards dissociation . . . in relationships between individuals, to inanimate objects, and to oneself. (p. 10)

The reporting of the Nazi war crimes trials, on the one hand, kept moving between these two poles both in Israel as well as in Germany. In other words, it was here and there occasionally driven by efforts to avoid or to suppress the past altogether. On the other hand, it was also driven by efforts to face and come to grips with the past. But the basic tendencies—the framing of the reporting concerning the Holocaust in each of the two countries—resided primarily close to one of the two poles of the continuum.

In Israel, the reporting of the Nazi trials—especially during the Eichmann trial and to some extent during the Demjanjuk trial—served to inform Israelis about the cruel past of their own people. This was accomplished above all through identifying with the victims; thus the historic events brought out during the trials became an important factor in the formation and maintenance of Israel's national collective identity. In the Federal Republic of Germany, on the other hand, Germans also came to terms with the Nazi past, at least in part via of the reporting about the trials, by trying to ward off the past through an effort to dissociate themselves from the German offenders. But however little one could strip the Nazi past, the democratic reconstruction of the German society required a break with the past, which the reporting about the Nazi trials helped to shape.

In Israel there seemed to be more identification. This may have been natural given the fact that the victims of the Holocaust were part of the people of Israel and because it is seemingly easier to identify with the victims than with the perpetrators. Because the perpetrators were German, they had to dissociate themselves from their own people, something which is seemingly not easy to do.

What evidence was found for identification in Israel? First and foremost, the Israeli news items were generally more salient than the German items: they were given greater prominence in the newspapers, they had wider and larger headlines, and in general their overall salience index was higher. There was also more emotion expressed in the Israeli items, although there was more emotion in the German headlines. As noted earlier, the photos that appeared in the Israeli newspapers were mainly of witnesses and had more to do with Holocaust in general and specifically with the death camps, and there was more mention and more details given of the atrocities. Finally, the condition and state of the survivors as well as the political climate and public opinion in Israel during the time the trials were being conducted was a more poignant issue in the Israeli press than in the German press. This latter point may suggest a link between the Holocaust and the present. The ability of people to incorporate the events of the Holocaust into current events may be indicative of the process of identification. By the same token, in the statements that appeared in the Israeli press there were more references to lessons to be learned from the Holocaust, which can also be considered as a sign of trying to incorporate what happened in the past with the current life of the people. And as noted, there was very little identification expressed in the German press.

What about dissociation in Germany? First and foremost, the overall coverage in the German press was relatively less extensive than in the Israeli press. As noted, the focus was more on the defendants, as can be noted from the photos and the greater mention of the characteristics and personality of the defendants. Finally, very pointedly, during the first three trials, that is, up until the end of the 1960s, the word "Holocaust" did not appear at all in the German press coverage.

Epilogue

The subject of the Holocaust is a difficult one to describe and discuss, especially when it involves the gruesome details of the merciless acts perpetrated by the Nazis against innocent victims. The decision to focus on trials of Nazi war criminals as portrayed by the press made the task somewhat more manageable, however. Relying on press reports made it possible to obtain information and insight, albeit second hand, pertaining to the societies in which they were published. In an age when the media rapidly develop and their role in shaping as well as reflecting public opinion and the public agenda is often taken for granted, there is special importance in studying their content in detail.

Although the coverage of Nazi trials in the press included much of the gory descriptions of the horrors of the period, as depicted by the prosecutors and the witnesses, this information by necessity went through filters created by newspaper editors in the selection of the materials to be presented, and by reporters in the way each and every one of them chose to provide the reader with their idiosyncratic context and interpretation. And yet, there should be little doubt that the way the press in Germany and Israel handled the coverage of the trials is indicative of the cultural, political, and social milieu in which the trials were conducted and in which the press operated.

The study reported in this volume has more or less covered the entire period in which most of the Nazi war crimes trials were conducted. The study encompassed four of the major trials, beginning with the

149

trials held in Nuremberg very shortly after the war and culminating with the Demjanjuk trial conducted in Jerusalem more than 40 years later. Surely a study of this nature, which examined in depth four major trials, could not deal with all the trials that took place during those decades. Furthermore, it would be wrong to assume that the press coverage of the trials presented all aspects of the Holocaust. In fact, many of the specific aspects that were sought in the coverage hardly appeared. This is the case because of the tendency of newspapers (as well as other media) to deal with the concrete here and now; thus, what was not said in the courtrooms or in connection with the trials would not be reported in the press.

It should also be noted, however, that with the conclusion of the Demjanjuk trial, trials of former Nazis did not come to an end. In fact, even today, as we turn the leaf into the 21st century, some trials are still going on and others are ending. In any event, stories concerning former Nazis accused of committing war crimes still make the news, albeit generally in the inside pages. For example, in 1998 Maurice Papon, a French citizen, then 87 years old, was tried in France for his part in the expulsion of 1,500 Jews from Bordeaux during World War II. In October 1999, Papon escaped to Switzerland just before the French court was about to sentence him, but he was subsequently arrested and extradited to France, where he has begun to serve a jail sentence.

As these lines are written, another suspected former Nazi criminal, Konrad Kalejs, aged 86, who had obtained Australian citizenship years ago, was deported back to Australia from the United Kingdom where he had been living. The British government had insisted that the police did not have enough evidence to arrest him (*New York Times*, January 7, 2000, p. 10).

In addition to the trials themselves, certain events that retroactively impinge upon the trials have recently surfaced on the public agenda. Thus, for example, Adolf Eichmann's son has petitioned the Israeli government to provide him with his father's diary, written while Eichmann was incarcerated during his trial in Jerusalem. The manuscript was kept under seal in the Israeli government archive and was not released to the public until the end of February 2000, following a debate that ensued as to who should have custody over the document.

It is also noteworthy that in recent years another intensive debate has been taking place, this time in Germany—somewhat reminiscent of the Historians' Debate of the mid-1980s—unleashed by Daniel J. Goldhagen's book *Hitler's Willing Executioners*, including a conflict between the novelist Martin Walser and Ignatz Bubis, the late president of the Central Jewish Council of Germany, and exacerbated by the plans and decision for the erection of a controversial Holocaust Monument in

Berlin, as well as by an exposition of the crimes of the former German Wehrmacht (Wilke, 1999). Here, too, the press has been serving as an important agent in the dissemination of these ideas.

Finally, most recently, the libel trial in London, in which British historian David Irving, author of about 30 books on World War II, lost the case in which he sued American history professor Deborah Lipstadt, for claiming that he was a Holocaust denier (*New York Times*, January 12, 2000, p. 7). This long-awaited trial has brought to the public agenda, once again, the claim by certain people that the Holocaust never happened. To help fight this allegation, the Israeli government immediately sent a copy of the above-mentioned Eichmann memoirs to Lipstadt's attorneys who had requested it (*Ha'aretz*, March 1, 2000).

The interesting point from the perspective of the current study is the fact that even more than half a century after the Second World War, when virtually all the trials of Nazi war criminals are over, the press has become the arena in which central issues pertaining to the Holocaust are being discussed, once again, this time at a level even further removed from the real events. Although the real events were not reported in real time, the press coverage of the trials served as a means of raising the issues. In the current libel trial it is very likely that documents and even testimony, court rulings, and judgements from previous Nazi war crimes trials—including those discussed in this volume—will be submitted, possibly together with some press reports, as part of the evidence for what did or what did not happen six decades ago. And yet, it seems that there is still public interest in such matters, and it is the press once again that serves as a vehicle to bring them to the fore.

At the same time, it seems that the subject of the Holocaust has also been receiving increased attention in cultural spheres, in film, theater, literature, and the arts as well as special commemorations by newly established museums and exhibits, including a new museum in Berlin, which will be opened in 2001. And all of these phenomena are naturally also reported, discussed, reviewed, and advertised in the press.

Although much of the cultural products concerning the Holocaust can be seen as some form of identification with the trauma and victims of the Second World War, some of these materials can also be interpreted, at least in certain circles, as a form of dissociation.

It has earlier been suggested that the presentation of the Holocaust in the media is indeed a complex and difficult task. These difficulties can also be described in terms of dissociation. Thus, for example, trivialization and instrumentalization tend to remove the media consumer from the real sense of the Holocaust. The various attempts that are made these days to popularize the Holocaust may turn out to be quite dangerous because they might provide a false sense that they are a new form of identification, whereas in essence they might be forms of dissociation (for example, it might be easier to deal with the Holocaust with a sense of humor, but by doing so people would dissociate themselves from the true essence of the issues). This creates a tough dilemma: in popular culture, where the expectations are to have everything instantly encapsulated, how can such a serious and somber message be transmitted from generation to generation? On the other hand, if not encapsulated, few would pay attention to it at all.

A case in point might be Roberto Benigni's 1998 film *Life is Beautiful*, in which a Jewish-Italian man and his young son are deported to a labor camp. In an attempt to cope with the horrors of life in the camp, the father and child develop a game-like routine that succeeds in saving the child's life. The fact that Benigni chose to deal with the Holocaust could be an indication of identification, but when closely examining the fantasy-oriented scenes and dialogues, reducing it to child's play, one might draw the false conclusion that Benigni's Holocaust is the Holocaust experienced by the real people during the 1940s in Europe. By presenting a farce, it could be argued, Benigni actually dissociates himself and his audience from the real meaning of the Holocaust.

In Israel in recent years the tendency for identification continues. This can be seen with the attempts to revive the memory of the Holocaust by sending high school students on trips to Poland, by bringing survivors to talk with students to recount their personal stories, and by assigning projects in which youngsters search for their roots using sophisticated data banks and computer technology. Grandparents tend to tell their grandchildren more than they told their children, so many new stories are still coming out. The concepts of the "Second Generations" and "Third Generation" are now becoming common terms.

Perhaps there is no other choice but to constantly move between the two polarities, going from identification to dissociation and back again in a vicious circle. It may also be that identification will take a different form than what has been the norm so far, as long as there are still survivors living in our midst as living proof to the atrocities and the victory of the human spirit over evil. But what will be considered as identification and when will the line be considered as having been crossed to dissociation is currently an open question that will have to be dealt with in the future as the Holocaust becomes a more remote event in history.

Appendix:
The Codebook of the
Content Analysis

#	Variable	Values
1	Newspaper	01. Frankfurter Allgemeine Zeitung 02. Frankfurter Rundschau 03. Nürnberger Nachrichten 04. Tagesspiegel 05. Süddeutsche Zeitung 06. Die Welt 07. Yediot Aharonoth 08. Ha'aretz 09. Davar 10. Herut 11. Hatzofeh 12. Hamashkif
2	Date	__ __ __ __ __ __ Day Month Year
3	Item ID	__ __ __ __
4	Trial	1. Nuremberg 2. Eichmann 3. Auschwitz 4. Demjanjuk

5	Source of item	1. Newspaper (unidentified)
		2. Journalist (byline)
		3. News agency
		4. Identified non-newspaper writer (e.g., politician)
		5. Other
6	Size of item	___ ___ ___ ___ ___ (in square centimeters)
7	Number of pages on which item appears	___ ___
8	Total number of columns across item	___ (maximum width)
9	Total number of Columns on page in which item appears	___
10	Beginning of item	1. First page, main headline
		2. First page, not main headline
		3. Special page, special section for the trial
		4. Supplement
		5. Other
11	Size of headline font	___ ___ (height in millimeters)
12	Use of direct quote in headline	01. No direct quote
		02. Yes, of the prosecution
		03. Yes, of the defendant
		04. Yes, of a victim witness
		05. Yes, of a non-victim witness
		06. Yes, of a judge
		07. Yes, of a defense lawyer
		08. Yes, of a German politician or public official
		09. Yes, of an Israeli politician or public official
		10. Yes, of a non-witness expert
		11. Yes, of a "man in the street"
		12. Other
13	Use of emotional term in headline	1. No
		2. Yes
14	Nature of item	01. News report
		02. Background article

03. Feature story
04. Editorial
05. Letter to Editor
06. Interview
07. Poll results
08. Documentation
09. Press citing other press sources
10. Photo/cartoon
11. Other

15	Nature of document	01. None

02. Indictment
03. Judgment
04. Prosecutor's argument
05. Defense argument
06. Transcript of witness testimony
07. Document presented to the court
08. Press conference
09. Speech regarding trial not in courtroom
10. Press comments
11. Documents regarding the trial but not presented to the court (e.g., personal letters)
12. Combination of the above

16	Illustration	1. None

2. One photo
3. Two photos or more
4. One cartoon
5. Two cartoons or more
6. Photos and cartoons

17	Size of first photo	__ __ __ __ (in square centimeters)
18	Subject of first photo	1. Trial: the defendant

2. Trial: the prosecution
3. Trial: defense attorney
4. Trial: witness(s)
5. Trial: judge(s)
6. Trial: courtroom or courthouse with persons
7. Trial: courtroom or courthouse without persons
8. Persons involved in trial but not present in courtroom
9. Scene of war crimes or the Holocaust

19	Size of second photo	__ __ __ __ (in square centimeters)
20	Subject of first photo	1. Trial: the defendant
		2. Trial: the prosecution
		3. Trial: defense attorney
		4. Trial: witness(s)
		5. Trial: judge(s)
		6. Trial: courtroom or courthouse with persons
		7. Trial: courtroom or courthouse without persons
		8. Persons involved in trial but not present in courtroom
		9. Scene of war crimes or the Holocaust
21	Size of third photo	__ __ __ __ (in square centimeters)
22	Subject of first photo	1. Trial: the defendant
		2. Trial: the prosecution
		3. Trial: defense attorney
		4. Trial: witness(s)
		5. Trial: judge(s)
		6. Trial: courtroom or courthouse with persons
		7. Trial: courtroom or courthouse without persons
		8. Persons involved in trial but not present in courtroom
		9. Scene of war crimes or the Holocaust
23	Stage of trial	01. Impossible to identify
		02. Pre-trial preparations
		03. Reading of indictment
		04. Opening speech by prosecution
		05. Testimony of the defendant
		06. Opening speech of the defense
		07. Testimony of witnesses
		08. Summation by defense
		09. Summation by prosecution
		10. Closing words of the defendant
		11. Verdict and opinions on verdict
		12. Sentencing and rationale for judgment
		13. Post-trial discussion and activities

Theme Analysis

24	The indictment	01. Preparation for war, warfare
		02. Economic plundering
		03. Discrimination against Jews
		04. Deportation, forced labor of Jews
		05. Extermination of Jews
		06. Discrimination against other people
		07. Deportation, forced labor of other people
		08. Extermination of other people
		09. Description of cruelties
		10. Explicit "crimes against humanity"
		11. Deportation of people of unknown identity
		12. Extermination of people of unknown identity
		13. Other
25	The proceedings	1. Preparation for the proceedings
		2. Handling of the proceedings
		3. Behavior of the defendant during proceedings
		4. Witnesses who committed crimes during Holocaust and who refuse to testify
		5. Evaluation of the verdict
		6. Other
26	Historical reasons	1. Political, economic and social situation before WWII
		2. Anti-Semitism
		3. German attitudes towards persecution of Jews (resistance and help)
		4. Other
27	Political situation during trial	1. Political atmosphere between Israel and Germany
		2. Public opinion in Israel
		3. Public opinion in Germany
		4. Public opinion in other countries
		5. New outbreaks of anti-Semitism
		6. Other
28	Moral aspect	1. Lessons to be drawn from the Holocaust

		2. Responsibility of the Germans for the Holocaust
		3. Other
29	Holocaust survivors	1. Life stories of Holocaust survivors
		2. Current condition of Holocaust survivors
		3. Other

Main point of item

30	The indictment	01. Preparation for war, warfare
		02. Economic plundering
		03. Discrimination against Jews
		04. Deportation, forced labor of Jews
		05. Extermination of Jews
		06. Discrimination against other people
		07. Deportation, forced labor of other people
		08. Extermination of other people
		09. Description of cruelties
		10. Explicit "crimes against humanity"
		11. Deportation of people of unknown identity
		12. Extermination of people of unknown identity
		13. Other
31	The proceedings	1. Preparation for the proceedings
		2. Handling of the proceedings
		3. Behavior of the defendant during proceedings
		4. Witnesses who committed crimes during Holocaust and who refuse to testify
		5. Evaluation of the verdict
		6. Other
32	Historical reasons	1. Political, economic, and social situation before WWII
		2. Anti-Semitism
		3. German attitudes towards persecution of Jews (resistance and help)
		4. Other

33	Political situation during trial	1. Political atmosphere between Israel and Germany 2. Public opinion in Israel 3. Public opinion in Germany 4. Public opinion in other countries 5. New outbreaks of anti-Semitism 6. Other
34	Moral aspect	1. Lessons to be drawn from the Holocaust 2. Responsibility of the Germans for the Holocaust 3. Other
35	Holocaust survivors	1. Life stories of Holocaust survivors 2. Current condition of Holocaust survivors 3. Other

Descriptive elements

36	Describing cruelties	1. None mentioned 2. Cruelties mentioned but not described 3. Cruelties described in detail
37	Number of victims	__ __ __ __ __ __ __ (code highest mentioned)
38	Witnesses	1. No mention 2. Biographical information mentioned 3. Biographical information and testimony 4. Evidence without mention of mental and physical condition 5. Mental and physical condition without evidence 6. Evidence and mental/physical condition 7. Evidence, mental/physical condition and bio data
39	Public interest in the trial in Israel	1. No mention 2. Specific mention of interest 3. Specific mention of no interest 4. Implication of interest (e.g., crowded courtroom) 5. Implication of no interest (e.g., no spectators in court)

40	Public interest in the trial in Germany	1. No mention 2. Specific mention of interest 3. Specific mention of no interest 4. Implication of interest (e.g., crowded courtroom) 5. Implication of no interest (e.g., no spectators in court)
41	Reactions in Israel towards Germany	1. No mention 2. Specified positive reaction 3. Specified neutral/ambivalent reaction 4. Specified negative reaction
42	Reactions in Germany towards Israel	1. No mention 2. Specified positive reaction 3. Specified neutral/ambivalent reaction 4. Specified negative reaction
43	Overall attitude on conducting trial	1. No mention 2. Positive attitude, for conducting trial 3. Negative attitude, against conducting trial 4. Both attitudes presented
44	Evaluation of emotional tone	1. No emotion 2. Low emotion (only few emotional terms used) 3. High emotion (more emotional terms used)
45	Specific expressions used in item	1. Holocaust 2. Race/racism 3. Anti-Semitism 4. Martyrdom 5. Heroism 6. Genocide 7. Extermination 8. Pogrom

Statement Analysis

46	Sources of statement	01. Author of the item 02. A judge 03. The prosecution 04. The defense 05. The defendant

06. A witness
07. An Israeli politician or public official
08. A German politician or public official
09. A foreign politician or public official
10. A non-witness expert
11. The Israeli public
12. The German public
13. Foreign public
14. The Israeli media
15. The German media
16. Foreign media
17. Unidentified source

47	Use of metaphors	

1. Like sheep to the slaughter
2. Old Testament reference
3. New Testament reference
4. Monsters
5. Animals (other than sheep)
6. Other

48	Reasons for conducting trial	

01. For the sake of justice (in a judicial sense)
02. As a moral obligation towards the victims
03. Revenge, recompensation
04. Deterrence, to prevent repetition
05. To come to terms with the past
06. To educate the young generation
07. To keep the past from disappearing into oblivion
08. As a way or reconciliation, atonement
09. To enhance Germany's current political situation
10. To enhance Israel's current political situation
11. To demonstrate Israel's power
12. To influence world public opinion
13. To demonstrate international law and its use
14. Other

49	Criticism towards the trial	

01. The public is not interested
02. Danger of trivializing the Holocaust
03. To put an end to the debates about the past

04. Trial brings back painful memories
05. Revival of animosities against Germans
06. Revival of anti-Semitism
07. How the defendant was brought to Israel
08. Statute of limitations
09. The right to conduct the trial
10. The legality of retroactive legislation
11. The inability of the judges to master all the material
12. The methods of investigation
13. Admissibility of documents
14. Trustworthiness of the witnesses
15. The way the proceedings are carried out
16. Sub-judice (pre-trial publication) issues
17. Other

50   Lessons to be drawn from the Holocaust

01. The need for tolerance towards minorities
02. The importance of democracy
03. The importance of Zionism
04. The moral responsibility to resist evil—limits to obedience
05. The importance of Jewish unity against modern anti-Semitism
06. Avoiding judgment when lacking common experience
07. Possibility of bravery through spiritual fortitude
08. The Holocaust is beyond comprehension
09. The danger of recurrence of the Holocaust
10. No lessons can be drawn from the Holocaust
11. Other

51   Legal aspects of the trial

1. The fundamental legal principals are sufficient
2. The proceedings are fair and just
3. Questioning the death penalty
4. Other

52	State of the defendant	01. The defendant is conscious of his guilt
		02. The defendant is not conscious of his guilt
		03. The defendant shows no reaction to testimony
		04. The defendant is embarrassed following testimony
		05. The defendant is apathetic or lacks feelings
		06. The defendant is arrogant, presumptuous
		07. The defendant seems to be a sadist
		08. The defendant seems to be a criminal
		09. The defendant committed the crimes of his free will
		10. The defendant committed the crimes to obey orders
		11. The defendant seems to be a typical German
		12. The defendant is not a typical German
		13. Other
53	Responsibility	01. There is collective guilt of the Germans
		02. There should be collective guilt of the Germans
		03. There is no collective guilt of the Germans
		04. There should not be collective guilt of the Germans
		05. There is collective shame of the Germans
		06. There should be collective shame of the Germans
		07. There is no collective shame of the Germans
		08. There should not be collective shame of the Germans
		09. German people knew about the persecution of the Jews
		10. German people didn't know about the persecution of the Jews
		11. It is not certain if German people knew about the persecution of the Jews

12. German people knew about the extent and/or nature of the Holocaust, especially the destruction of the Jews
13. German people didn't know about the extent and/or nature of the Holocaust, especially the destruction of the Jews
14. It is not certain if German people knew about the extent and/or nature of the Holocaust, especially the destruction of the Jews
15. There were Germans who tried to help
16. There were no Germans who tried to help
17. The Germans are responsible for the results of the Nazi era
18. The Germans are not responsible for the results of the Nazi era
19. Jews in Palestine knew about the extent and/or nature of the Holocaust
20. Jews in Palestine didn't know about the extent and/or nature of the Holocaust
21. It is uncertain whether or not Jews in Palestine knew about the extent and/or nature of the Holocaust
22. The Western world knew about the extent and/or nature of the holocaust
23. The Western world didn't know about the extent and/or nature of the Holocaust
24. It is uncertain whether or not the Western world knew about the extent and /or nature of the Holocaust
25. Other

| 54 | Reasons for the Holocaust | 1. Historic reasons: Development of Germany since the nineteenth century
2. Economic conditions
3. National character: Nature of the German people
4. National character: Nature of the Jewish people
5. Loss of religious ties |

		6. Cultural decline 7. Decay of the political order 8. Anti-Semitism 9. Other
55	Anti-Semitism	1. Anti-Semitism is regarded merely as an historical phenomenon 2. Anti-Semitism is regarded as a current problem 3. Anti-Semitism is regarded as both an historical and a current problem 4. Other
56	Analogies of the Holocaust	Every statement that compares the Holocaust to other events should be coded in connection with its sources (e.g., the Armenian and the Cambodian tragedies).
57	Evaluation of the judgment	1. It is a sign of justice 2. It is not just because the punishment is too severe 3. It is not just because the punishment is too mild 4. There is no proper punishment for such crimes 5. Other

References

Adoni, H., & Mane, S. (1984). Media and social construction of reality: Towards an integration of theory and research. *Communication Research, 11,* 323-340.

Arendt, H. (1963). *Eichmann in Jerusalem: A report on the banality of evil.* New York: Viking Press.

Ariel, Y. (1961). *The Eichmann trial as mirrored by the Neo-Nazi press.* Jerusalem: Yad Vashem (Hebrew).

Asa, T., & Dgani, A. (1991). Voluntary delegations to Poland: Approval and refusal. In D. Bar-On & A. Sela (Eds.), *Psychosocial effects of the Holocaust on the second and third generation* (pp. 131-177). Beer Sheba: Ben-Gurion University Press (Hebrew).

Baldwin, P. (Ed.). (1990). *Reworking the past. Hitler, the Holocaust, and the historian's debate.* Boston: Beacon Press.

Bar-On, D. (1994). *Fear and hope.* Tel Aviv: Ghetto Fighters' House and Hakibbutz Hameuhad Publishers (Hebrew).

Bar-On, D., & Sela, A. (1991). *"The vicious circle": Between reference to reality and reference to the Holocaust among Israeli youth.* Beer Sheba: Ben-Gurion University (Hebrew).

Bauer, Y. (1982). *A history of the Holocaust.* New York: F. Watts.

Bauer, Y. (1990, April). *The influence of the Holocaust on the Israeli society.* Lecture delivered for the "Holocaust Seminar," the Hebrew University, Jerusalem.

Bauer, Y., & Lowe, M. (1981). Introduction. In Y. Bauer & N. Rotenstreich (Eds.), *The Holocaust as historical experience* (pp. vii-xiv). New York: Holmes and Meier.

Bergmann, W., & Erb, R. (1990). Neue Perspektiven der Antisemitismusforschung. In W. Bergmann & R. Erb (Eds.), *Antisemitismus in der politischen Kultur nach 1945* (pp. 11-18). Opladen: Westdeutscher Verlag.

Bergmann, W., & Erb, R. (1991). "Mir ist das Thema irgenwie unangenehm." Kommunikationslatenz und Wahrnehmung des Meinungsklimas im Fall Antisemitismus. *Kölner Zeitschrift fur Soziologie und Sozialpsychologie, 43*, 502-519

Bier, J. P. (1986). The Holocaust, West Germany, and strategies of oblivion, 1947-1979. In A. Rabinbach & J. Zipes (Eds.), *Germans and Jews since the Holocaust. The changing situation in West Germany* (pp. 185-207). New York: Holmes and Meier.

Bosch, W. J. (1970). *Judgement on Nuremberg: American attitudes toward the major war crime trials.* Chapel Hill: The University of North Carolina Press.

Brochhagen, U. (1994). *Nach Nürnberg. Vergangenheitsbewältigung und Westintegration in der Ära Adenauer.* Hamburg: Jumius.

Browning, C. R. (1992). German memory, judicial interrogation and historical reconstruction: Writing perpetrator history from postwar testimony. In S. Friedlander (Ed.), *Probing the limits of representation: Nazism and the "final solution"* (pp. 22-36). Cambridge, MA: Harvard University Press.

Carlebach, E. (1985). *Zensur ohne Schere. Die Gründerjahre der "Frankfurter Rundschau" 1945/47.* Frankfurt am Main: Röderberg-Verlag.

Carmichael, J. (1961). Reactions in Germany (The Eichmann case). *Midstream, 7*, 13-27.

Caspi, D. (1986). *Media decentralization: The case of Israel's local newspapers.* New Brunswick, NJ: Transaction.

Caspi, D. (1988). The Holocaust as a political-communication dilemma. *Otot, 96* (June), 22, 65 (Hebrew).

Caspi, D., & Limor, Y. (1999). *The in/outsiders: Mass media in Israel.* Cresskill, NJ: Hampton Press.

Dayan, D., & Katz, E. (1992). *Media events: The live broadcasting of history.* Cambridge, MA: Harvard University Press.

Dekoven-Ezrachi, S. (1980). *By words alone: The Holocaust in literature.* Chicago: University of Chicago Press.

Deutsch, A. W. (1974). *The Eichmann trial in the eyes of Israeli youngsters.* Ramat Gan: Bar Ilan University Press.

Dohrendorf, R. (1990). *Zum publizistischen Profil der "Frankfurter Allgemeinen Zeitung."* Frankfurt am Main: Lang.

Doneson, J. E. (1985). *The Holocaust in American film.* Unpublished doctoral dissertation, the Hebrew University, Jerusalem.

Doob, A. N., & Macdonald, E. (1979). Television viewing and fear of victimization: Is the relationship casual? *Journal of Personality and Social Psychology, 37,* 170-179.

Eckhardt, A., & Eckhardt, R. (1978). Studying the Holocaust's impact today: Some dilemmas of language and method. *Judaism, 27,* 222-232.

Eisner, J. P. (1983). The genocide bomb: The Holocaust through the eyes of a survivor. In R. L. Braham (Ed.), *Perspectives on the Holocaust* (pp. 149-163). Boston: Kluwer-Nijhoff.

Elias, N. (1983). *Engagement und Distanzierung. Arbeiten zur Wissensoziologie I.* Frankfurt: Suhrkamp.

Farago, U. (1984). Holocaust consciousness among Israel high school youth, 1983. *Holocaust Research Papers, 3,* 159-178.

Fischer, H. D. (1966). *Die grossen Zeitungen: Portraits der Weltpresse.* München: Deutscher Taschenbuch Verlag.

Frei, N. (1992). Auschwitz und Holocaust. Begriff und Historiographie. In H. Loewy (Ed.), *Holocaust: Die Grenzen des Verstehens. Eine Debatte über die Besetzung der Geschichte* (pp. 101-108). Hamburg: Rowohlt.

Friedlander, S. (1977). *Some aspects of the historical significance of the Holocaust.* The Philip M. Klutznick International Lecture, Institute of Contemporary Jewry, Hebrew University of Jerusalem.

Friedlander, S. (1984). *Reflections of Nazism: An essay on kitsch and death.* New York: Harper and Row.

Funkenstein, A. (1989). The theological interpretations of the Holocaust: A balance. In F. Furet (Ed.), *Unanswered questions: Nazi Germany and the genocide of the Jews* (pp. 275-303). New York: Schocken Books.

Gerbner, G., & Gross, L. (1976). Living with television: The violence profile. *Journal of Communication, 26,* 172-199.

Gillessen, G. (1986). *Auf verlorenen Posten. Die Frankfurter Zeitung im Dritten Reich.* Berlin: Siedler.

Giordano, R. (1987). *Die zweite Schuld oder Von der Last Deutscher zu sein.* Hamburg: Rasch und Roehring Verlag.

Glock, C. Y., Selznick, G. J., & Spaeth, J. L. (1966). *The apathetic majority. A study based on public responses to the Eichmann trial.* New York: Harper and Row.

Grabitz, H. (1988). Problems of Nazi trials in the Federal Republic of Germany. *Holocaust and Genocide Studies, 3,* 209-222.

Grabitz, H. (1994). Die Verfolgung von NS-Verbrechen in der Bundesrepublik Deutschland, der DDR und Oesterreich. In R. Steininger (Ed.), *Der Umgang mit dem Holocaust* (pp. 198-220). Wien: Böhlau.

Guri, H. (1963) *The glass cage*. Tel Aviv: Hakibbutz Ha'meuhad Press (Hebrew).

Hamerman, A. (1986). The Demjanjuk trial: Deja vu. *Politics, 8*, 12-13 (Hebrew).

Hausner, G (1968). *Justice in Jerusalem*. New York: Schocken Books.

Herman, S. (1977). *Jewish identity*. Beverly Hills, CA: Sage.

Herman, S., Peres, Y., & Yuchtman, E. (1965). Reactions to the Eichmann trial in Israel: A study of involvement. *Scripta Hierosolymitana, 14*, 98-118.

Hohenberg, J. (1969). *The professional journalist: A guide to the practices and principles of the news media* (2nd ed.). New York: Holt, Rinehart and Winston.

Hurwitz, H. (1972). *Die Stunde Null der deutschen Presse. Die amerikanische Pressepolitik in Deutschland 1945-1949*. Köln: Verlag Wissenschaft u. Politik.

Institut für Demoskopie Allensbach (1960). Die Stimmung im Bundesgebiet Nr. 453: Der Fall Eichmann.

Institut für Demoskopie Allensbach (1961). Allensbacher-Archiv, IfD-Umfrage 923: Antisemitismus.

Institut für Demoskopie Allensbach (1986). Allensbacher-Archiv, IfD-Umfrage Nr 3394: Deutsche und Jeden vier Jahrzehnte danach.

Institut für Demoskopie Allensbach (1992). Allensbacher-Archiv, IfD-Umfrage Nr 5068.

Institute of Human Relations (1962). *The Eichmann case in the American press*. New York: Author.

Kampe, N. (1987). Normalizing the Holocaust? The recent historians' debate in the Federal Republic of Germany. *Holocaust and Genocide Studies, 2(1)*, 61-80.

Katz, E. (1973). Culture and communication in Israel: The transformation of tradition. *The Jewish Journal of Sociology, 15*, 5-21.

Katz, E., & Gurevitch, M. (1973). *The culture of leisure in Israel*. Tel Aviv: Am-Oved (Hebrew).

Katz, E., Haas, H., Gurevitch, M., Weitz, S., Adoni, H., & Goldberg, D. (1992). *The culture of leisure in Israel: Changes in cultural activity patterns 1970-1990*. Jerusalem: Israel Institute of Applied Social Research and the Ministry of Education and Culture (Hebrew).

Keren, N. (1985). *The influence of public opinion leaders on the one hand and Holocaust research on the other hand on the development of educational discourse and curricula concerning the Holocaust in Israeli high schools and informal education (1948-1981)*. Unpublished doctoral dissertation, Hebrew University, Jerusalem (Hebrew).

Kittel, M. (1993). *Die Legende von der "Zweiten Schuld." Vergangenheitsbewältigung in der Ära Adenauer*. Berlin: Ullstein.

Klein, D. (1987). Self-exonerating memories. *Dimensions, 3*(1), 3.

Klüger, R. (1992). *Weiter leben: Eine Jugend.* Göttingen: Wallstein Verlag.

Koszyk, K. (1986). *Pressepolitik für Deutsche 1945-1949* (Geschichte der deutschen Presse Part IV). Berlin: Colloquium Verlag.

Kruse, F. (1978). NS-Prozesse und Restauration. Zur justitiellen Verfolgung von NS-Gewaltverbrechen in der Bundesrepublik. *Kritische Justiz, 2,* 108-134.

Less, A. (1987). *Schuldig. Das Urteil gegen Adolf Eichmann.* Frankfurt am Main: Athenaeum.

Levy, S. (1985). *Components of the Jewish identity as motivators for Jewish identification among Jewish youth and adults in Israel in the period 1967-1982.* Unpublished doctoral dissertation, Hebrew University, Jerusalem (Hebrew).

Liebman, C.S., & Don-Yehia, E. (1983). *Civil religion in Israel. Traditional Judaism and political culture in the Jewish state.* Berkeley, CA: University of California Press.

Lipstaft, D. E. (1986). *Beyond belief: The American press and the coming of the Holocaust 1933-1945.* New York: The Free Press.

Lübbe, H. (1985). Verdrängung? Über eine Kategorie zur Kritik des deutschen Vergangenheitsverhältnisses. In H. A. Strauss & N. Kampe (Eds.), *Lerntag uber den Holocaust in der politischen Kultur seit 1945* (pp. 50-60). Berlin: Technische Universität.

Maassen, L. (1986). *Die Zeitung. Daten-Deutungen-Porträts.* Heidelberg: Müller.

Maier, C. S. (1988). *The unmasterable past: History, Holocaust, and German national identity.* Cambridge, MA: Harvard University Press.

Marcuse, H. (1987). West German strategies for commemoration. *Dimensions, 3*(2), 13-14.

Marshall, B. (1980). German attitudes to British military government 1945-47. *Journal of Contemporary History, 15*(4), 655-684.

McCombs, M. E., & Shaw, D. L. (1972). The agenda setting function of the press. *Public Opinion Quarterly, 36,* 176-187.

Mendelssohn, P. (1959). *Zeitungsstadt Berlin. Menschen und Mächte in der Geschichte der deutschen Presse.* Berlin: Ullstein.

Merritt, A., & Merritt, R. L. (Eds.) (1970). *Public opinion in occupied Germany.* The OMGUS-Surveys 1945-1949. Urbana: University of Illinois Press.

Mitscherlich, A., & Mitscherlich, M. (1991). *Die Unfähigkeit zu trauern.* München: Piper.

Molotch, H., & Lester, M. (1974). News as purposive behavior. *American Sociological Review, 39*(1), 101-112.

Naumann, B. (1965). *Auschwitz. Bericht über die Strafsache gegen Mulka und andere vor dem Schwurgericht Frankfurt.* Frankfurt: Fischer.

Nir, R., & Roeh, I. (1992). Intifada coverage in the Israeli press: Popular and quality papers assume a rhetoric of conformity. *Discourse and Society, 3*(1), 47-60.

Nossek, H. (1994). The narrative role of the Holocaust and the state of Israel in the coverage of salient terrorist events in the Israeli press. *Journal of Narrative and Life History, 4*, 119-134.

Ozick, C. (1969). The uses of legend: Elie Wiesel as Tzadik. *Congressional Bi-Weekly, 36*(9), 19.

Papadatos, P. (1964). *The Eichmann trial*. London: Stevens.

Porat, D. (1986). *An entangled leadership*. Tel Aviv: Am-Oved (Hebrew).

Prittie, T. (1967). *Israel: Miracle in the desert*. New York: Praeger.

Renn, W. (1987). Mastering the past: A report from Germany. *Dimensions, 3*(1), 4-8.

Rivers, W. L. (1975). *The mass media reporting, writing, editing*. New York: Harper and Row.

Robinson, J. (1965). *And the crooked shall be made straight*. New York: Macmillan.

Rosen, K. H. (1985). Der Holocaust und die politische Kultur der Bundesrepublik Deutschland. In H. A. Strauss & N. Kampe (Eds.), *Lerntag über den Holocaust in der politischen Kultur seit 1945* (pp. 61-72). Berlin: Technische Universität.

Rückerl, A. (1979). *The investigation of Nazi crimes 1945-1978: A documentation*. Heidelberg: C. F. Müller.

Ryan, C. (1991). *Media strategies for grassroot organizing*. Boston: South End Press.

Schmidt, R., & Becker, E. (1967). *Reaktion auf politische Vorgänge. Drei Meiningsstudien aus der Bundesrepublik*. Frankfurt: DIVO.

Segev, T. (1993). *The seventh million*. New York: Hill and Wang.

Segev, T. (1994a). *Journalism and history*. Lecture given at the Hebrew University on June 12th.

Segev, T. (1994b). Personal interview with T. Zemach, July 31st.

Shandler, J. (1999). *While America watched: Televising the Holocaust*. New York: Oxford University Press.

Sheftel, Y. (1994). *The Demjanjuk affair: The rise and fall of a show-trial*. London: Gollancz.

Sontag, S. (1966). Reflections on the deputy. In S. Sontag, *Against interpretation*. New York: Dell.

Startt, J. D., & Sloan, W. D. (1989). *Historical methods in mass communications*. New Jersey: Erlbaum.

Steinbach, P. (1981). *Nationalsozialistische Gewaltverbrechen in der deutschen Öffentlichkeit nach 1945*. Berlin: Colloquium Verlag.

Steinbach, P. (1984). Zur Auseinandersetzung mit nationalsozialistischen Gewaltverbrechen in der Bundesrepublik Deutschland. Ein Beitrag zur deutschen Kultur nach 1945. *Geschichte in Wissenschaft und Unterricht, 35,* 65-85.

Stock, E. (1954). The press of Israel: Its growth in freedom. *Journalism Quarterly, 31,* 481-490.

Strothmann, D. (1984). Statements zu Prozessberichterstattung und Bewusstseinsbildung-der Beitrag der Medien. In J. Weber & P. Steinbach (Eds), *Vergangenheitsbewältigung durch Strafverfahren? NS-Prozesse in der Bundesrepublik Deutschland* (pp. 192-206). Munich: Olzog.

Taylor, T. (1992). *The anatomy of the Nuremberg trials. A personal memoir.* New York: Knopf.

Teicholz, T. (1990). *The trial of Ivan the Terrible: State of Israel vs. John Demjanjuk.* New York: St. Martin's Press.

Vidal Naquet, P. (1989). Theses on revisionism. In F. Furet (Ed.), *Unanswered questions: Nazi Germany and the genocide of the Jews* (pp. 304-319). New York: Schocken Books.

Wagenaar, W. A. (1988). *Identifying Ivan: A case study in legal psychology.* Cambridge, MA: Harvard University Press.

Weber, J. (1968). Sinn und Problematik der Nürnberger Kriegsverbrechenprozesse. *Aus Politik und Zeitgeschichte* (Supplement to the weekly newspaper). *Das Parlament, 48,* 3-31.

Weimann, G., & Winn, C. (1986). *Hate on trial: The Zundel affair, the media and public opinion in Canada.* Oakville, Ontario: Mosaic Press.

Wiesel, E. (1978). *A Jew today.* New York: Random House.

White, H. (1992). Historical emplotment and the problem of truth. In S. Friedlander (Ed.), *Probing the limits of representation* (pp. 370-53). Cambridge, MA: Harvard University Press.

Wieland, W. (1991). Ahndung von NZ-Verbrechen in Ostdeutschland 1945 bis 1990. *Neue Justiz 45,* 49-53.

Wilke, J. (1994). Press. In E. Noelle-Neumann, W. Schultz, & J. Wilke (Eds.), *Fischer Lexikon Publizistik/Massenkommunikation* (pp. 382-417). Frankfurt: Fischer.

Wilke, J. (1999). Massenmedien und Vergangenheitsbewältigung. In J. Wilke (Ed.), *Mediengeschichte der Bundesrepublik Deutschland* (pp. 649-671). Köln: Böhlau.

Wolffsohn, M. (1993). *Eternal guilt? Forty years of German-Jewish-Israeli relations.* New York: Columbia University Press.

Yablonka, H. (1994). *Foreign brothers: Holocaust survivors in the state of Israel 1948-1952.* Beer Sheba: Ben-Gurion University (Hebrew).

Young, J. E. (1993). *The texture of memory: Holocaust memorials and meaning.* New Haven, CT: Yale University Press.

Zimmermann, M. (1994). Israels Umgang mit dem Holocaust. In R. Steininger (Ed.), *Der Umgang mit dem Holocaust-Europa-USA-Israel* (pp. 387-406). Vienna: Böhlau.

Zimmermann, M. (1992). Die Folgen des Holocaust fur die israelische Gesellschaft. In *Aus Politik und Zeitgeschichte* (Supplement to the weekly newspaper). *Das Parlament*, Section B1-2, pp. 33-43.

Zuckermann, M. (1993). *Shoah in the sealed room: The "Holocaust" in Israeli press during the Gulf War*. Tel Aviv: Author.

Author Index

Subject Index

179

Codebook of content analysis, 153-165
Coding procedure, 56, 88
Cognitive dissonance, 145
"Collective silence," 24
Column width of items, 77, 79-81, 154
Commission Against Anti-Semitism, 29
Content analysis, 39-40, 51-52
    codebook of, 51-52, 153-165
    time frames for, 51
Continuity of coverage, 60-63
Coverage
    continuity of, 60-63
    overall, 58-60
Crimes
    statements about responsibility for, 121-124
Criminal Proceedings Against Mulka and Others, 18
Criticism of the trials
    `statements about, 114-117, 161-162
Cronkite, Walter, 12
"Cultivation hypothesis," 5

D

DANA news agency, 71
Davar, 47-48
Defendants, 141
    statements about characteristics of, 108-111
Demjanjuk trial, 2-3, 6-7, 9, 19-22
    journalistic context of, 19-22
Der Tagesspiegel, 43-44
Deutsche Allgemeine Nachrichtenagentur, 12
Die Welt, 45-46
Dissociation and identification, 137-48, 152
DIVO Institute, 27

E

Ehrenburg, Ilya, 12
Eichmann trial, 2, 6-7, 9, 13-17
    journalistic context of, 13-17
Emotional tone of the items
    in press coverage of trials, 134-135, 154, 160
Evaluation of the verdicts
    statements about, 125, 129-130
Extent of coverage of the trials, 57-65
    continuity of, 60-63
    overall, 58-60
    space allocated to, 63-65
Extent of the items
    in press coverage of trials, 57-65

F

Frankfurter Allgemeine Zeitung, 46
Frankfurter Rundschau, 43
Free trials, 6
Freedom of the press, 6

G

German newspapers studied, 43-46
    Der Tagesspiegel, 43-44
    Die Welt, 45-46
    Frankfurter Allgemeine Zeitung, 46
    Frankfurter Rundschau, 43
    Nurnberger Nachrichten, 44-45
    Suddeutsche Zeitung, 44
German newspapers studied, 43-46
German society
    Holocaust and, 23-29
Germany
    Nazi, 1
Goldhagen, Daniel J., 150
Guilt
    relative interpretations of, 111
Guri, Haim, 15